# BOOMS, BUSTS & BUSHFIRES

# BOOMS, BUSTS & BUSHFIRES

1973–

JACKIE FRENCH

ILLUSTRATIONS AND CARTOONS BY

PETER SHEEHAN

An Omnibus Book from Scholastic Australia

*To Mark, Julian and Margrete, and wonderfully talented Peter, who brought this series forth, with enormous gratitude for their patience, insight, knowledge and wisdom; and to the idealists, larrikins and all those who worked to make our nation good. – JF*

Omnibus Books
an imprint of Scholastic Australia Pty Limited (ABN 11 000 614 577)
PO Box 579
Gosford NSW 2250
www.scholastic.com.au

Part of the Scholastic Group
Sydney • Auckland • New York • Toronto • London • Mexico City
• New Delhi • Hong Kong • Buenos Aires • Puerto Rico

First published by Scholastic Press in 2011.

Illustrations and cartoons by Peter Sheehan.
Cover design by Lake Shore Graphics.
Internal design and typesetting by Lake Shore Graphics.

A catalogue record for this book is available from the National Library of Australia

ISBN: 9781742762517

Typeset in 11.5/15pt Esprit Book.

Printed by McPherson's Printing Group, Maryborough, VIC.

Scholastic Australia's policy, in association with McPherson's Printing Group, is to use papers that are renewable and made efficiently with wood from responsibly managed sources, so as to minimise its environmental footprint.

The paper in this book is FSC® certified. FSC® promotes environmentally responsible, socially beneficial and economically viable management of the world's forests.

21 22 23 24 25 / 2

# CONTENTS

# A HUNGER TO KNOW MORE

History is mostly made up of what people think is important to remember. But what was most important about the past 40 years?

So far, the seven books in this series have had other history books to guide them, as well as the type of official material that is released after 50 years, when it can no longer affect the people or organisations it mentions. There were collections of diaries, letters and memoirs, too.

This eighth book covers a period that is too recent for some of that material to be available. More than any of the other books, I have had to rely on my own memory, as well as newspaper accounts that do not tell the full story. I have also had to choose not what I think is most important about the past 40 years, but what readers might feel they should know about. (If this was my own story of the past 40 years, it would be a book about humanity's destruction of the planet, at the same time as we begin to glimpse an understanding of the universe and ourselves.)

Perhaps someone writing a history of these times 50 years from now will talk about them as the last years before humans colonised the stars, or survived without computer-enhanced brains, or perhaps lived in the relative calm before the great resource wars. We rarely know what the future will see as important about our own times.

It has felt strange knowing that, even though I've lived through many of the events in this book, I may know less about what truly matters than I do about the more distant past.

No history book can ever tell the whole story. There is too much the writer or illustrator doesn't know. But with *Booms, Busts and Bushfires*, as with the other Fair Dinkum Histories, I hope you feel that you have begun to know the history of our nation—and that we've given you a hunger to know more.

# CHAPTER 1

# A LUCKY SUNBURNT COUNTRY

Australia had changed before, but slowly—with hot, dry periods that lasted for years, decades, even thousands of years; with the slow spread of Indigenous nations across the continent, and the faster, but still gradual, spread of the colonisers after 1788.

Now everything seemed to speed up. So many changes had occurred in the US, the UK and Europe during the 1960s—all of them watched every night in Australian lounge rooms on the television news—that some people spoke of the 60s as a decade of social revolution. Different ways of thinking, new inventions and changing fashions still mostly came from overseas, but communications and travel brought information to Australians faster than ever before. Once we had been at the end of the world. Now, with cheap plane tickets and TV, we no longer seemed so far away.

Japan's economy had grown rapidly since the World War II and they needed Australia's mineral resources. The 1960s mining boom meant that Australia was a wealthier nation than ever before—although, as usual, not everyone had a share of the wealth.

Affluence meant that more people had a chance of getting a good education and a well paying job. It was a confident time—and the optimism helped to increase the rate of change, too. Young people demanded that they be allowed to do things their way, instead of dutifully doing whatever their parents told them to.

Skirts were short and hair was long. Young people wore fringes that strayed into their eyes. Even men had hair down to their collars or shoulders. Only old men or 'dags' still had short-back-and-sides hair. Sometimes girls wore long dresses even in the day time—'maxi' dresses or cheap colourful printed skirts from India, with bright cotton shoulder bags.

The 'fab four' British pop group the Beatles became interested in the spiritual leader of the Transcendental Meditation movement, the Maharishi Mahesh Yogi. In 1967 and 1968 they studied meditation with him in Wales and in India. Soon it seemed everyone was wearing Indian clothes, sandals and jewellery, listening to sitar music and burning sticks of incense.

At the same time, the hippies in California began to express their opposition to the war in Vietnam with the slogan 'Make Love, Not War'. They called themselves the 'flower children', marched in the streets for peace and believed that flower power could be stronger than firepower. They dreamt of living in communes, where all possessions were shared. Some even did it.

Even those who didn't share the hippy philosophy shared the 'flower child' fashions. Kids put flower stickers on their schoolbags and books. On the weekend even men wore floral printed shirts from India, and Monday to Friday their business shirts were pink or blue—so different from the starched white ones they had worn only a few years before. Sometimes they even went to the office without a tie! Everyone was searching for a simpler, less formal life.

So it was a relaxed and hopeful time—for Australians, anyway. World War II and the Great Depression were long gone. Australian wool and minerals had made the country wealthy. Most people aimed to have a three-bedroom house on a nice block of land, with lots of flowers and shrubs instead of the fruit trees and vegetable gardens of their parents. There were often three kids, a dog, a cat, a car for Dad and—just maybe—one for Mum, too.

Only ten years earlier, most women had been homemakers ('housewives'), or were waiting to be married. Now new universities were built in the suburbs and women were encouraged to study either full-time or part-time. And they were allowed to qualify as doctors, dentists or lawyers, although few did.

Most men, and even women themselves, were still wary of consulting women professionals—and it was unthinkable for a woman to be a mechanic or a plumber, or to fly a passenger plane. Many places wouldn't hire married women and, even in the public service, married women weren't regarded as permanent employees, so they didn't get superannuation or other benefits. Women still earned much less money, although they might be doing exactly the same job as a bloke.

But now at least school girls were choosing careers—even if they planned to work only till the kids were born. Almost as many girls as boys were getting a driver's licence. And lots of women were becoming stroppy and demanding the same rights and wages as men. On top of that they wanted time off to have babies! Feminism, the Women's Movement, Women's Lib—it had several names—was encouraging women to think that they had more options than ever.

Impossible. Or was it?

So much had changed so fast. Only ten years earlier most families had gathered around the radio or read together, while Mum got the dinner and Dad worked in his shed at the end of the day. Now nearly everyone had a TV and watched the same mostly British or American shows right across the country.

But above all, it was a time of dreams. Nearly everyone was sure that life would keep on getting better—though there were lots of very different ideas about what the wonderful world of the future should look like. Medical scientists could stop kids dying or being paralysed by polio and other terrors that used to kill nearly half the children before they reached the age of five. The first human heart was transplanted in 1967 and in 1969 the first 'small step' was taken on the moon.

Maybe in a few more years we'd all have robot servants, take holidays on the moon, or fly in our own jet-powered cars. Maybe we'd achieve something even greater—a peaceful Earth, with no more prejudice or war, where no child died of starvation or preventable diseases and everyone could go to a doctor and sleep in a comfortable bed.

But along with the shared hope that made so many want to change the world, there was shared fear, too. For the past 20 years or more, the adults of the 1970s had lived with the threat of a nuclear war between the two superpowers—the United States and the Communist USSR, who were locked in a constant opposition referred to as the 'Cold War'. Instead of fighting each other openly in a third world war, they took sides in many smaller conflicts. With Australia as one of its strongest allies, the US was still supporting the fight against Communism in Vietnam, and although the governments of the USSR and China were very different from each other, the fact that no western country recognised Communist China meant that the Russians and the Chinese were lumped together as being 'Communist'.

Another fear was slowly building, too—the worry that humans were poisoning the planet. In 1962 US marine biologist Rachel Carson had written a book called *Silent Spring*, about a world where there were no birds left to sing, because chicks had failed to hatch as their eggshells had been thinned by DDT and other pesticides. The English magazine the *Ecologist* brought the word 'ecology' into common use by students and others who studied the complex interrelationships among living things and the natural environment, and saw alarming signs that human beings were disturbing the ecological balance.

In 1968 American astronaut William Anders took a photograph of Earth that was to become known as 'Earthrise' and then in 1972 the crew of Apollo 17 took photographs that made Earth look like a beautiful big blue marble. Lots of kids had a poster of one of these pictures on their bedroom wall. The photos reminded us that we were a single planet—incredibly beautiful and fragile. And in 1974 an American TV show for kids called 'The Big Blue Marble' was launched and was seen in many countries for the next nine years. Like 'Sesame Street', it emphasised the importance of living and working happily together as people who shared a single world. Australia might have been 'down under', at one end of that world, but we were part of it all.

Or were we right down the bottom? Back in the 50s Aussie kids learnt English history, rather than Australian; in the 60s kids learnt a bit about our own land, too. But now in the 70s there was a slow realisation that we weren't some European outpost, far away from any familiar countries except New Zealand, which had a similar history and culture. We had simply never paid much attention to our geographical neighbours.

Australians were finally noticing the neighbourhood.

## Part of Asia?

The idea that we were really part of Asia or one of the Pacific nations was still ridiculous to most Australians. We were Europeans, no matter where our continent was located. But slowly this was beginning to change.

One reason was the war in Vietnam. Refugees desperate for freedom and safety sailed in leaky little wooden boats to northern Australia. Many Australians were worried that there'd be a flood of these 'boat people'. They thought these people were merely economic refugees, who wanted to live in a richer nation and hadn't really been at risk of losing their lives at all. But most were found to be genuine refugees, without a land they could safely go home to. Nor were there very many of them, after all—just a few thousand. This was tiny compared with the number of illegal immigrants who arrived by plane on tourist visas and didn't go home.

Still, some politicians were able to exploit old fears in the non-Indigenous population that Australia would be invaded from the north. This was bitterly ironic to some Indigenous Australians, who pointed out that Europeans invading in the 18th century were in fact the first 'boat people'.

The new arrivals came from many backgrounds. Often their qualifications weren't recognised in Australia and at first their English wasn't very good. But they all had traditions of good food—food that was quite different from the sort eaten by most Australians at the time. They opened restaurants that served exotic and delicious meals very cheaply. And their popularity changed things for earlier generations of immigrants, too. The Chinese who had been here for over a century, but mostly cooked 'Australian Chinese'—chicken with almonds, sweet and sour pork with red food colouring—now found that Australians wanted to learn about the real variety of Chinese regional cuisine. We learnt that there was more to Italian food than pizzas and spaghetti, that Greek didn't just mean moussaka, or Russian food borscht and blini.

Women's magazines featured the food of one country after another. The *Australian Women's Weekly* famously cooked every recipe three times in their test kitchens before it was published, so Australians could experiment without fear of failure. Each recipe was still slightly changed for Australian tastes and the ingredients that were available, but by the end of the 70s we had so many more choices. Mum's traditional roast lamb was now a treat that the family ate a few times a year, instead of every week.

And if we weren't eating the poor old lamb, we weren't wearing its wool as often, either. Now you could buy clothes made in Taiwan, Indonesia and India that were even cheaper than the fabric you'd have needed to buy if you wanted to make them. Jumpers were no longer knitted by your Aunt Ethel or your gran. They were made on machines far away, from yarn that had never been anywhere near a sheep.

## What's for dinner?

The number of choices was greater than it had been ten years earlier, but there was so much of everything too! The new shopping centres with their big new supermarkets—and trolleys that held far more than Mum's basket or string bag used to—were packed with groceries laid out in brightly lit rows. It was so easy to pick up and buy all sorts of things that you'd never bought before and often didn't really need.

People did still eat the food of the countries their families had come from. If your gran came from England or Ireland you ate mashed potatoes; if she came from China you ate rice; if she came from Greece you ate baklava, even if you wanted the jam donuts or cream buns from the tuck shop at school. Cautiously, the supermarkets began to offer some of the ingredients for Australians to experiment with the foods of other traditions, but the owners were far more interested in selling them the new mass-produced 'convenience foods'.

Chicken raised in battery farms and then frozen didn't taste of much, but now it was the cheapest meat around, instead of being a treat for Christmas and birthdays, as it had been in the past. There were new frozen foods, too, such as fish fingers—crumbed oblongs that tasted vaguely like fish mixed with old oil. There were frozen beans and frozen peas, so you no longer had to sit and push them from their pods. And flakes of dried potato that you added hot water to and didn't even have to mash.

The idea of a 'treat' started to change, too. You could have ice-cream every day, instead of once in a blue moon when the ice-cream man drove along your street on a hot day, ringing his bell. It wasn't the creamy stuff of a few years earlier and it was made from powdered milk and artificial flavours. But it was cold and sweet—and cheap. There were all kinds of frozen ice-blocks too, and packets of chips and biscuits.

There were washing machines that cleaned your clothes and spun them dry, so you no longer had to boil them in a copper or push them through rollers (a mangle) to get the water out before you hung them up. You could get a lawnmower with a motor, so you didn't have to push a hand mower around the yard, and some even had grass-catchers attached, so you didn't need to rake the clippings or bend over to pick them up. You could get a 'mixmaster' to make your cakes; a refrigerator and even a deep freezer to store enough frozen food for months. You could buy an iron that spat out steam to help smooth out the wrinkles in your clothes. There were indoor toilets in all cities and towns and even in many farming areas—with seemingly endless rolls of pink or blue toilet tissue, instead of scratchy squares of old newspaper.

But Australia wasn't a land of plenty for everyone.

## The Dispossessed

If you were a single mum, only charity or help from family and friends could keep your kids fed and clothed, as there was no single mother's benefit. Really bright kids could get scholarships to go to university and there were jobs for everyone now, so there was plenty of part-time work to help you survive. But unless you got a scholarship, your family had to be well off to afford uni fees, especially if they had more than one kid. In those days, most Australian families had at least three kids—and in those days they'd still choose to spend money on educating their sons, rather than their daughters. Why bother, when daughters ended up getting married anyhow?

There were pensions for old people, but they didn't provide enough money to live on comfortably. And what if you got sick? It cost a lot to go to the doctor—except in Queensland, where public hospitals were free, though you might wait six hours to see a doctor or nurse.

And for Indigenous people things were even worse. Many whites wouldn't give them a job, let them drink in a hotel, or even serve them in a shop. There were few schools or doctors and nurses in remote areas, where many Indigenous people lived. But their situation was unseen and unheeded by most Australians.

Did Australia have to be like this, though? Could the nation change and really provide a fair go for everyone? The Labor Party fought the 1972 election with the theme 'It's Time'.

They won—and the effect was dramatic.

# CHAPTER 2

# 'IT'S TIME!'

For many people this was the most exciting time since Australia had floated north from Antarctica, about 84 million years earlier.

After 23 years of conservative government—mostly under one prime minister, Sir Robert Menzies—the Australian Labor Party led by Gough Whitlam had finally won an election. They had promised a different Australia—and that was what they helped to create.

For years, committees of academics and other experts had been working on ways to reshape Australia for the better. More new ideas were made law in a short time than ever before in this country.

## EDWARD GOUGH WHITLAM

Gough Whitlam was a giant of a man. He towered over just about everyone else in the room except his wife, Margaret, who was almost as tall and had a wit and a fierce intelligence to match her husband's. The cartoonists saw his height as symbolic. In any gathering of world leaders he was unlikely to be overlooked: Australia and its prime minister had to be noticed. He was one of the most dramatic prime ministers ever to lead the country and an extraordinary public speaker. In 1972 he spoke at election rallies, urging Australians to change, under the banner 'It's Time'. The ALP's campaign centred on a video clip that featured famous actors and musicians, all happily singing the jingle 'It's Time'—a new American-style marketing of politics, where advertising was important, and the feel of the ad meant more than what it actually said.

The lyrics said it was time for young people, time for old people, time to care about Indigenous rights, time to give every Australian access to high quality health care and education. For a generation of voters who had grown up with folk music and political anti-war rock lyrics, the words of 'It's Time' echoed those of the song 'Turn, Turn, Turn', which had been a hit for both Pete Seeger and the Byrds in the 60s. And that song, in turn, was based on the words of *Ecclesiastes* chapter 3, in the *Bible*, which begins 'To everything there is a season, and a time to every purpose under heaven.'

So this election jingle was powerful stuff. Whitlam had a vision of what Australia could be, and the determination and extreme self-confidence to feel he could change an entire nation.

It almost worked.

Edward Gough Whitlam was born in July 1916 in the Melbourne suburb of Kew. His father, HFE Whitlam, was Commonwealth Crown Solicitor and Australia's representative on the United Nations Human Rights Commission. Gough grew up in a household that asked questions, read widely and cared deeply about human rights. He graduated in law from Sydney University in 1946 and became a barrister in 1947. In 1952, he won the seat of Werriwa for the ALP in a federal by-election.

Idealistic young Australians flocked to Canberra to be part of this new world. Many returned from overseas jobs. Australian companies were given preference for government contracts. So great was the pressure on Canberra's rental market that huge queues formed outside real estate agents' offices, hours before they were due to open their doors.

Public servants were often rattled by the new recruits, who were full of ideas for change and had little time for the hierarchical nature of the old public service.

Almost every day a new wide-ranging change was put into place: Whitlam abolished conscription—the 'lottery' that sent young men to fight the war in Vietnam—and brought the remaining Australian troops back from Vietnam. Young men who were about to be conscripted, and the families and girlfriends who loved them, wept as they heard him announce that conscription was over. Our armed services would be made up of those who had chosen to defend Australia, not those forced into battle by the fall of a lottery ball.

From early colonial days to World War II, Australia had looked to England to defend us, and to tell us who was a friend and who was the enemy—even when the enemy was far away, like the Turks at Gallipoli, and had never threatened Australia. Since World War II, though, we had depended upon the United States and followed them into the Korean War and then Vietnam.

Now Gough Whitlam thundered that we were part of Asia. During the election, he did away with the formal British 'Ladies and gentlemen' and began his address 'Men and women of Australia'. Once elected, he did away with the terms 'Commonwealth Government' and 'Federal Government' and referred only to 'The Australian Government'. The Australian government was one of the first in the world to recognise China. (The US and other major countries were still trying to pretend that the government of Taiwan, which had been ruling China when Mao Zedong's armies forced them out, were still the real rulers of the world's largest nation).

Whitlam made personal visits to Indonesia in September 1973 and to six south-east Asian nations including the Philippines in 1974—unheard of for any prime minister before him. In 1973 Papua New Guinea was made self-governing and moved towards the granting of full independence from Australia in 1975.

The Whitlam government changed Australia's idea of who we were—not tenants in an outpost of Europe at the bottom of the world, relying on the UK or the US for everything from movies to foreign policy, but men, women and children of our own nation with our own culture—a nation of many cultures merging to form a unique identity.

**1973:**
**IMAGES OF OURSELVES**
Patrick White became Australia's first winner of the Nobel Prize for Literature. After so many years and so much controversy, on 20 October the Sydney Opera House was opened. It immediately became symbolic of a new Australia.

For nearly 200 years new settlers had mostly been white and English-speaking. Six years before the 1972 election victory, however, the Holt government had significantly revised Australia's immigration policy to include highly qualified people who would otherwise have been ineligible on account of their ancestry and skin colour. In 1973, the Whitlam government abolished the White Australia policy by removing race as a factor. Now applicants of any cultural origin were eligible to become citizens after three years of permanent residence.

The new word to describe this policy was 'multiculturalism'. There were grants for festivals to celebrate the history, the arts and food of the diverse cultural backgrounds of many Australians; there were grants for language teaching and cultural studies in universities and schools. And with the Racial Discrimination Act in 1975 it was against the law to discriminate on the basis of race, colour or national origin.

## The Australia Council

Reshaping the culture by changing the ways Australians saw themselves was not restricted to the Whitlam government's multicultural project. The Australia Council was set up in 1973 to centralise funding for the arts generally.

It made grants to Australian writing, visual arts, music and performance. Art galleries were funded with a dollar from the government for every dollar they spent on artworks by living Australian artists. And in 1973, the government bought the controversial painting 'Blue Poles' by the US artist Jackson Pollock for the Australian National Gallery. At $1.3 million, the most expensive painting at the time, and many Australians were outraged by what they saw as a waste of money on a meaningless canvas covered in paint dribbles. Others felt encouraged that the government was making a symbolic statement of support for the arts and Gough Whitlam put 'Blue Poles' on his Christmas card. Forty years later, the painting is estimated to be worth 200 times the purchase price, so whichever way you look at it, it wasn't a bad investment.

Also in 1973, the Australian Film and Television School was established, and in 1975 the Australian Film Commission followed, to ensure that not everything Australians saw on TV and at the movies would be from the US or the UK. Australia had been one of the first countries to produce feature length films in the early 20th century, but distributors of US films helped to kill off the local industry. Now Australia was a centre for filmmaking again. In 1974 Gough and Margaret Whitlam even agreed to appear as themselves in the Barry Humphries feature film 'Barry McKenzie Holds His Own'. At the end of the film, the prime minister bestows a mock honour on the character of Mrs Edna Everage and makes her a Dame. Having the prime minister play even a cameo role in a commercial film was regarded as frivolous by the government's critics, but others enjoyed the acknowledgment of the popular arts and Whitlam's sense of humour.

Only a few years earlier, most of the people who were serious about working as actors, writers, musicians or artists had gone overseas, at least till they had established their reputations. Suddenly there were lots of Aussie TV shows, films and plays. Writers were able to write full-time. And Australian artists who had gone overseas to work came back home to be part of the excitement. It was an incredible flowering of Australian creativity and the results are still with us today.

Some of the Whitlam government's achievements were very, very practical, like the extension of the sewerage system to outer Sydney and Melbourne, and putting in proper sewerage systems in many other parts of the country. (It was about time!) But other changes were grander in scale. University fees were abolished, so that every Australian who could pass the entrance exams was able to go to university.

And by mid-1975 every Australian was covered by a health insurance scheme, Medibank. Visits to the doctor or the hospital were heavily subsidised and often free. Women were at last given equal pay for equal work, and it was illegal to sack a woman just because she'd married. Elizabeth Reid was appointed in 1973 as special adviser on women's affairs to work with the prime minister and in 1974 an Office of Women's Affairs was set up in the Department of Prime Minister and Cabinet to look after issues of particular interest to women.

The voting age was reduced from 21 to 18. Whitlam reckoned if you were old enough to fight in a war, you were old enough to vote on whether the country should go to war or not. And in 1975 the Family Law Act changed the whole idea of marriage for life, by introducing the principle of no-fault divorce. Now you could obtain a divorce if you had lived apart for a year and could show that your marriage had broken down. Property was divided equally, or went to those who needed it most to care for the kids. The courts now recognised that a woman who'd looked after the kids instead of working in a paid job deserved an equal share of property after a divorce. The Family Court was set up in 1975, too, to help solve disputes.

The government created a Department of Aboriginal Affairs and established the Aboriginal Land Rights Commission in February 1973, headed by Justice Woodward, to find out the best way to recognise Indigenous land rights. The first federal Department of Environment and Conservation brought in the idea of 'environmental impact statements'—looking at what effect a proposed development would have on the environment before a project could be approved.

But Gough Whitlam and senior ministers including Tom Uren, Lance Barnard, Rex Connor and Jim Cairns had even grander visions for Australia. They dreamt of big projects, such as a gas pipeline running right across the country, and they wanted to force overseas companies to pay world prices for timber and minerals, instead of the ridiculously cheap deals they'd had up till then.

## The Inland Sea Again?

On 31 January 1974, floods covered about three quarters of Queensland, including large areas of Brisbane—partly because Brisbane City Council had allowed new houses to be built in places that had been flooded many times before. Floods also covered large tracts of New South Wales, Victoria and the Northern Territory. The dry and salty expanse of Lake Eyre in South Australia turned into a real inland sea, covered with bird life...for a while.

Instead of overcrowded capital cities, businesses and families would move to regional centres such as Albury-Wodonga and Bathurst-Orange. Regional commissions were set up to administer grants, instead of giving money through the state governments. Some even thought the state governments would slowly vanish, and leave just one Australian government for the whole country and local governments to deal with practicalities closer to people's homes. (The state governments and state public servants didn't like this idea at all, but people still talk today about Australians being over-governed.)

There were so many changes and policies aimed at creating a better Australia that it would take many books to detail them all. All Australians would have equal opportunity and for every problem there would be a solution…

But one of the biggest changes of all was the acknowledgement that Australia's history hadn't begun when Captain James Cook sailed up the east coast in 1770, and that Indigenous Australians had rights to their own land.

**Cyclone Tracy**
25 December (Christmas Day), 1974, Cyclone Tracy struck Darwin. Nearly half the city's residents were left homeless and buildings were reduced to piles of twisted metal and rubble. Most of Darwin's population was evacuated down south till the city could be rebuilt.

## Land Rights

At the beginning of 1972 the Aboriginal Tent Embassy was pitched in front of Parliament House, Canberra. It was a way of telling the world that in this town of embassies representing sovereign nations, Australia's Indigenous people were claiming rights to their own land and that they felt they needed an embassy to represent their interests to the Australian government.

The Woodward Commission's findings would eventually lead to the Aboriginal Land Rights (Northern Territory) Act 1976 under Prime Minister Malcolm Fraser and the establishment of an elected National Aboriginal Consultative Committee.

In August 1975, Gough Whitlam emptied a handful of central Australian soil into the hand of Vincent Lingiari of the Gurindji people at Wattie Creek, Northern Territory and formally handed over title deeds to a part of the Gurindji traditional lands. The Gurindji, who had been workers on the Vestey's cattle property Wave Hill, had gone on strike in 1966. The Vestey Group was a privately owned company from Britain that was involved in the meat trade. Now Whitlam was symbolically saying that he would make sure the land was recognised as Gurindji country.

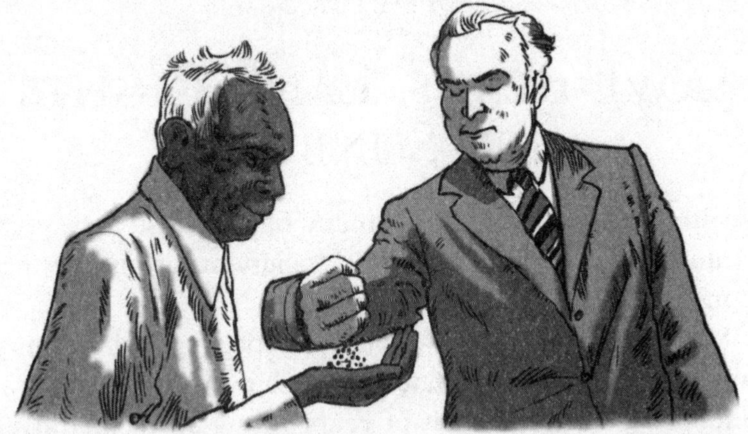

All this meant that land rights was an issue non-Indigenous Australians now had to think about, rather than dismiss as irrelevant to them, because Indigenous lands had been taken by other people a long time ago. During the 70s, 80s and 90s this change in thinking led to the establishment of independent Indigenous land rights bodies, such as the Northern Territory's Northern and Central Land Councils and Western Australia's Kimberley Land Council, and to land rights legislation that was drafted in other states.

## Chapter 3

# Love Beads, Land Rights and Sunburn

Wealth and the war in Vietnam had in different ways created a totally new 'alternative' society in various western countries, including Australia.

Many young Australians were questioning their parents' values. Some rejected materialism, big business and war completely. For thousands of years young people had lived with their parents till they married; even then they often stayed with one lot of parents till they bought or built their own home—or never left at all.

Now more kids than ever before were leaving home after school to share houses or flats with other young people, many of them in groups big enough to split the rising cost of renting a house in the capital cities. They were even (Shock! Horror!) living with their girlfriends or boyfriends before they got married.

Only a decade earlier young people weren't supposed to even think about sex before they got married. (Most did think about it, of course. They just kept it quiet.) Now couples had 'trial marriages' to see if they could stand living together before they actually got married.

When 'the pill' (the first oral contraceptive) arrived in 1960, many thought it would lead to immoral behaviour and a breakdown of families. Others saw it as a further way of liberating women by letting them choose when to have children. The idea of couples living together instead of getting married first shocked lots of older people. But as so many young people started to do it, most got used to it pretty fast.

But some young people were making even greater changes in their lives than simply leaving their parents' homes.

## NIMBIN

With all the focus on affluence and comfort in the 50s and the 60s, it seemed that the average person's greatest ambition had been to own a new TV set, a bigger car, a bigger house, a new white fridge…

Young people who had grown up with the physical security of that time, but with the threat of war between the USSR and the United States as well, wanted a world of peace and simplicity. They were also critical of the connections between materialism and defence spending—for example the way that big corporations made a lot of money out of equipping a country for war.

The hippie movement had started in California in the 1960s, but Australian young people (and some not so young) took to it, too. Some hippies lived in communes in city houses—not just sharing the house, but sharing everything they owned. Others longed for land in the country, where they could be self-sufficient—grow their own food without chemicals, build their own homes with solar or wind power systems and get back to nature. Even more, they dreamt of what they called an alternative society, modelled on traditional tribal societies around the world, where everyone cooperated and shared. They envisioned an Australia in which a few examples of alternative living could so inspire people that more and more would 'drop out' and mainstream life in the cities would wither away.

But few young people had the money to get land—or the knowledge to work it, but they didn't know that yet. In 1973, the Australian Union of Students (AUS) decided to get the alternative society going and chose the Nimbin Valley, a dairying area hidden in the hills behind Lismore and Murwillumbah in northern NSW, as the place. The soil was fertile there, the rainfall high and land prices were low. Dairying was hard work and poorly paid, so farmers were often eager to sell their land. And Nimbin was too far from any big city for holiday homes. It was also very beautiful.

Why students? There were lots of them, thanks to the increased funding of universities under the Menzies government, and the abolition of fees by Whitlam. They were studying new developments in education and politics and they had grown up with television and were beginning to study the influence of mass communication. Australian students in the 60s and 70s were watching international events daily by satellite, and images of (if not the reasons for) the 1968 general strike in France. The student riots in Paris encouraged them to think they could throw off the old ways of their parents and create a social revolution.

Inspired by 1969's Woodstock Festival in the United States, the Nimbin experiment would start off with a week-long counter culture Back to the Earth celebration, called the Aquarius Festival. People played music, sang and danced. But they also talked. And when the majority of partygoers went back to their studies or jobs in the cities, a few idealists stayed, to club together and buy land, build their homes, plant their gardens—and found a new society.

The Tuntable Falls Co-ordination Co-operative bought 486 hectares for $100,000 and sold 500 shares for $200 each.

In those days the basic male weekly wage was $50. So for a month's work you could buy the right to share in a big bit of land: a place to build your house and change your life. Other co-operatives including Paradise Valley Pastoral Company and Nmbngee Community Co-operative were also begun (and all three are still in existence, although not quite in the same framework as when they began).

All over Australia other alternative communities began to grow, usually on abandoned farming land, often with soil erosion and full of weeds, but cheap to buy.

The gardens withered in the drought at the end of the 70s. The dome houses—supposed to be the cheapest, most efficient form of housing, so different from the nation's suburban boxes—leaked and cracked and were invaded by mice and mozzies. The hippies found that you couldn't dig potatoes in bare feet and cheesecloth shirts or dresses.

Many of these new settlers stayed just a few years, then went back to live in towns or cities, especially when they had kids who needed to go to school. But others learnt to wear boots and farm gear and acquired the skills needed to live in the bush. And they passed their ideals on to others.

It was the hippies who worked out how to farm and garden organically—without pesticides and herbicides—and many of their techniques are used on farms today. It was the hippies who worked out alternative ways of getting electrical power from the sun and wind—the technologies the world is turning to now, with the awareness of global warming. Hippies became artists, wood workers, writers and film makers and did change Australia, though not in the way they thought they would back in 1973.

It's easy to dismiss the hippies as airheads who thought that sexual freedoms, drug-taking and a bit of cheesecloth would create a new world. Today Nimbin land prices are high—you need to be a millionaire to drop out there now—and most of the communes didn't last long. But they didn't fail, either. They ended up as legal ways for people to have their own bit of land and share in common land…rather like city people who have their own apartment in a block of flats with communal areas. But there are still organic markets, the Rainbow Power company and other businesses run by idealists, and thousands of Australians who have never been to Nimbin, in small yet definite steps forward, are also working to change the ways we think and live.

# Slip, Slop, Slap

We were the land of the 'bronzed Australian'. You hadn't enjoyed a decent summer holiday unless you came back so sunburnt that your skin peeled off in strips. (The kid in the row behind you at school could make the maths class more interesting by pulling the strips of papery dead skin off your back.) In the 1950s nearly all men smoked and a lot got drunk most nights, too. As women gained greater equality with men at home, in the workplace and schools, they started to smoke as well. Tobacco companies exploited the women's movement with images of women who had the right to wear pants to the office and smoke in the street. The trouble was that both too much sun and cigarettes led to cancers.

But in the 1970s, public health campaigns really got going. Kids were urged to 'slip, slop, slap'—slip on a shirt, slop on sunscreen, slap on a hat. Cigarettes had to be packaged with health warnings to show just how smoking resulted in cancer, harmed babies, caused wrinkles, or led to heart disease and death. Black tars were squeezed from lungs on television advertisements, often around mealtimes.

And the new campaigns worked, slowly but surely. Every year fewer Australians smoked, and more slopped on sunscreen instead of the baby oil that they had slathered themselves with in the 60s so they could tan more quickly. Any Australian kid who had worn a shirt or a hat to the beach in the 50s was either a redhead with pale skin or a wuss. Tanning had been linked to longstanding cultural images of a healthy outdoors life and cigarette advertisers had connected smoking with sports and masculinity. They were part of the story of what it was to be Australian. So this change in such a short time was remarkable. But the thing that cut down drinking was the breathalyser.

The breathalyser—a device for measuring how much alcohol is in your blood by measuring how much is in your breath—was first used in New South Wales in 1969. All through the 1970s random breath tests were used increasingly, along with advertising campaigns to stop people drinking and driving. And to counter the impression that only falling down drunks were a danger behind the wheel, the term 'drink driving' was introduced. *Any* amount of drinking was a potential problem: you didn't have to be 'drunk'.

It worked. Although there may always be people who drink too much then get into the driver's seat, the Australian tolerance of heavy drinking changed within a few years. People had one glass now, instead of eight or ten. If anyone planned a big night out they arranged for a 'designated driver' or ordered taxis. But more than anything else, for the first time since the Rum Corps and illegal stills in the early colony of New South Wales, the way Australians drank alcohol changed. The days of blokes stopping at the pub, drinking as much as they could, then rolling home drunk were over.

## CHAPTER 4

# LABOR GETS THE BOOT

Change was making Australia a more equal and secure place, with opportunities for the majority.

But all this change scared people, too. Many Australians felt that some people—like students, single mothers, artists and those who were unemployed—were getting a lot for nothing. And their taxes were paying for it. They had been used to the Liberal-Country Party government for 23 years and the same prime minister, Robert Menzies, for most of that time. They liked to call Whitlam a 'traitor to his class'. Apparently, a man with that kind of profession and education should have been on the conservative side of politics! To some, including many in the public service, this new lot didn't seem like a real government at all.

On 16 March 1973 the Attorney-General, Lionel Murphy, ordered the Commonwealth Police to raid the Melbourne headquarters of the Australian Security Intelligence

Organisation, ASIO. He believed that ASIO wasn't showing the government vital intelligence on the Croatian right-wing extremists in Australia, who were (possibly) planning to infiltrate the Australian army, train supporters and collect arms to fight back home in Eastern Europe. There were also rumours that ASIO was still keeping watch on government ministers, especially their links with any Communist country, as though Labor wasn't really the government at all. After all, the Labor government had recognised Communist China—what else might they get up to? The raid caused much criticism of the new government in the media and unease among many about this so-called invasion of Australia's spy agency. In August 1973, Gough Whitlam admitted that the Murphy raid was the greatest mistake of his government's nine months in office.

The new government's move into areas like regional development and education, formerly the preserve of the states, resulted in Labor and non-Labor states attacking the Australian government's erosion of states' rights. Other conservative lobby groups, like much of the medical profession, who were unsettled by the moves to set up Medibank, also started to turn to the conservative opposition.

And the Whitlam government wasn't able to pass all the laws it wanted to, either. Although Labor had gained a majority in the House of Representatives in 1972, it never had a majority in the Senate. The opposition blocked a number of major pieces of proposed legislation and the Senate rejected 93 bills—more than the total number rejected during the previous 71 years.

But the real problem was money.

The new medical cover for everyone, the free education, the money spent on giving every town and city sewerage instead of backyard dunnies or big tanks that polluted the rivers and beaches—all these developments cost a lot.

The Australian government was spending so much that inflation grew. In December 1972 the annual rate of inflation was 4.5 per cent. Before the end of 1973 it was 10 per cent and by June 1974 it had soared to 14.4 per cent.

Unemployment was also rising. People's wages doubled, but even that wasn't enough to compensate for high interest rates, when they tried to borrow money to buy a house, a car or manufactured goods from overseas.

Whitlam sensed that people were becoming nervous about the rate of change and the money being spent, particularly on welfare and grants to the arts. Some people felt that working in the arts was a hobby, not a real job, and that taxpayers' money was being wasted on frivolous pursuits.

The Labor government's desire to support the disadvantaged revived the term 'dole bludger' and there were stories about people going to the doctor when they didn't need to, just because it was free.

But Whitlam hoped that enough people shared his vision of Australia to give Labor control of the Senate as well as the House of Representatives. For a bill to become law it had to be passed by both houses of parliament, and if he didn't have enough senators to support his legislation, his continuing program of change wouldn't get through.

He called an early election on 18 May 1974—long before the end of the three-year term Labor had been elected for. His aim was partly to show that the people of Australia really were behind his changes, and also to get enough Labor senators elected so all the new laws would be passed. It was a double dissolution—that is, both houses of parliament were up for election.

To maintain continuity and stability, normally only half the senators are up for election. But if the Senate keeps rejecting bills passed up to it from the House of Representatives, then the prime minister can dissolve both houses of parliament and ask the voters of Australia to decide whether they want to increase their support for the government, or change it.

Australians confirmed their support for the government. But instead of a majority of 13 in the House of Representatives, they only had a majority of five after the election, even though they'd got just under 50 per cent of the vote—the same as in the previous election.

How did this happen? Australia is divided into electorates, or districts, based on population for the purposes of voting for the House of Representatives. Voting for the Senate is based on the states. Every state has an equal number of senators (the territories now have two each), and all voters in the state choose them. But when it comes to the House of Representatives, Australians vote only for a representative of their own electorate—and no electorate has exactly the same number of voters. Back then many country electorates had less than half the number of voters that the big city electorates had—so it was as though some Australians had two votes.

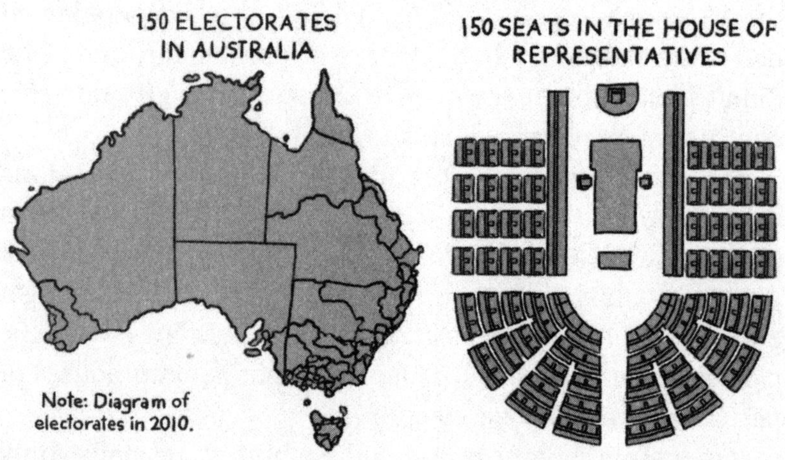


Labor was back in—but still with too few senators to give them the power to pass many of their bills. The big new plans to put a gas pipeline across Australia, a train system all the way to Darwin instead of just to Alice Spings, new roads and new universities and technical colleges were all going to cost even more money.

# The Loans Affair

Minerals and Energy Minister Rex Connor was an idealist, a tough, belligerent, but kind and also generous man, who would work himself to death trying to make sure Australia's mineral bounty brought money to Australia, instead of selling it at the ridiculously low prices that had been negotiated before. He wanted to 'buy back' Australia—get at least 51 per cent Australian ownership for all companies exporting our minerals, so that at least half the profits would stay in this country. He planned to fund a natural gas pipeline, electrify railways across the country and fund uranium enrichment. Connor had the government's support and tried to get a $4 billion and then a $2 billion loan for his plans.

But permission was revoked, as the government was already deeply in debt. White-faced and trembling, but still a giant stroppy old man, in parliament Connor thundered a poetic rebuke based on the words of the American Sam Walter Foss:

*Bring me men to match my mountains,*
*Bring me men to match my plains,*
*Men with empires in their vision,*
*And new eras in their brains.*

Despite failing health, Connor forced himself to keep going and secretly kept looking for ways to fund his schemes, even though he had no parliamentary approval to do so. He approached a London-based commodities trader named Tirath Khemlani, to see if he could set up a loan.

The secret negotiations were leaked to the Liberals by Khemlani as it later turned out, then to the press, and treasurer Jim Cairns misled parliament over the affair. It was an enormous scandal. Exactly what had been going on? Whitlam dismissed both ministers as a result, but the affair energised those who believed this government was inexperienced, incompetent and was spending too much. The fact that Khemlani was Pakistani and was sourcing loans in the Middle East also revived old prejudices among some Australians.

**Rex Connor was an idealist, a bit of a loner and an eccentric. Minister for Minerals and Energy 1972-75, he never spoke to journalists. He died in 1977.**

(Media watch: the author acknowledges bias here. As the most junior graduate clerk in Rex Connor's department, I was given the opportunity to write part of a background briefing for him. Usually such a briefing was anonymous, or circulated in the name of the person of higher rank who presented it. But Connor wanted to know exactly who had written what. He sent back a message, 'Tell her thank you, good work'—an unknown politeness and consideration from a minister. The next day I watched him struggle to stay upright as he walked—or staggered—up the steps to a meeting with a Japanese delegation, physically supported by his permanent secretary. Connor knew his heart was failing. He knew he would die if he kept working. He was a tough old battler who loved this country.)

## The Dismissal

The new Liberal Party leader, Malcolm Fraser, cited the loans scandal as a reason for exploiting the opposition's majority in the Senate. The opposition refused to pass the budget bills in the Senate, in an attempt to force the government to hold yet another election.

**Not a Good Omen**

**5 JANUARY 1975.**
**Part of the Tasman Bridge crossing the River Derwent in Hobart collapsed, when struck by the bulk ore carrier, MV Lake Illawarra, which sank, killing seven crew members. Twelve people were killed—five trapped as their cars sank in the river.**

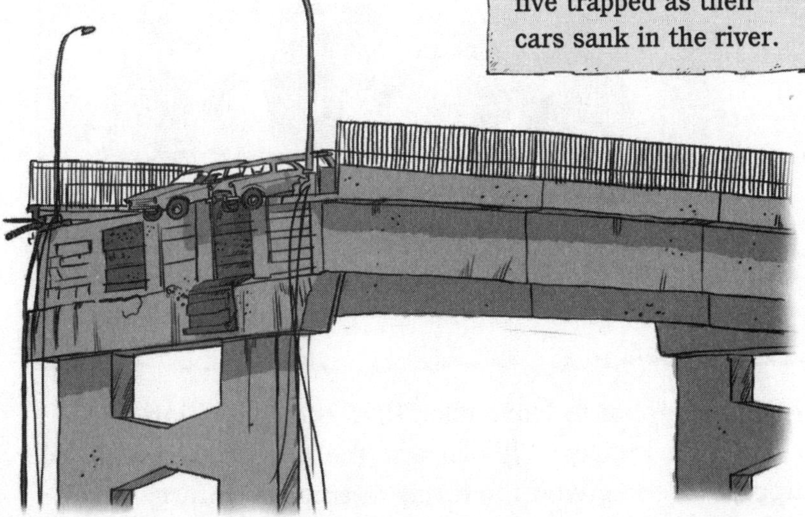

Whitlam had gone to the people early last time in 1974, but he wouldn't go again—partly because the loans affair had been damaging. It was all too likely his government wouldn't win another election, especially so soon after the last one.

## The Balibo Five

### 16 October 1975

**Five Australian TV newsmen were killed by Indonesian forces during the Indonesian invasion of East Timor. Although many Australians felt a bond with the Timorese, who had sheltered and protected many soldiers from the Japanese in World War II, Prime Minister Gough Whitlam's government did not condemn the invasion, and took little action to find out exactly how and why the newsmen had been killed. It would be decades before their families had answers and the true story may still not be known.**

From October to November 1975 the opposition refused to pass the budget. This meant the government had no 'supply' vote to give it the funds to run the country.

Who was going to win? Would Fraser really let the government go broke, so that it couldn't pay any pensions, wages or bills? Or would Whitlam give in and call an election after all? The parties were deadlocked. Fraser went to the governor-general, Sir John Kerr, and asked him to intervene.

Ironically, Whitlam had recommended the appointment of Sir John Kerr to the Queen. He had also replaced the imperial honours system with the new Order of Australia in February 1975, and had had the Queen proclaimed 'Queen of Australia' to end the symbolism of the Queen as a foreign head of state. Commentators later observed that the Queen had not intervened in the constitutional crisis, but her Australian-born representative had agreed to do so, and controversy over several aspects of his decision continues decades later.

On 11 November the governor-general used the lack of 'supply' as a reason to dismiss Whitlam and his government. And he appointed Malcolm Fraser as caretaker prime minister until elections could be held.

Gough Whitlam became the only Australian prime minister to be removed from office and his government the only one that had a majority in the House of Representatives, but was not allowed to govern. On the afternoon on 11 November, a shocked and furious Whitlam stood on the steps of the old Parliament House in Canberra before a crowd that had gathered as the news of the dismissal flashed around the city.

'Well may we say "God Save the Queen",' he thundered. 'Because nothing will save the governor-general.' He urged the crowd and all Australians to 'maintain the rage' over his dismissal. There was plenty of rage—but not enough electoral support for a government that many felt was sending the country bankrupt.

Malcolm Fraser won the election on 13 December 1975 with an overwhelming majority. The ALP won only 36 seats, while the Liberal Party won 68 and the National Party 22.

The days of the grand vision were over.

# The Queen's Man?

Sir John Kerr remained as governor-general until his resignation in 1977. But although Australians had voted Whitlam out, public opinion still viewed Kerr's actions as sneaky. He was publicly ridiculed, especially after he appeared drunk in public at the Melbourne Cup, and caricatured for his outdated wearing of a top hat. He was appointed Australia's ambassador to UNESCO. But this was seen as a thank you and, because of the great public outcry, he never took up the job. He died in 1991.

# The End of a Vision

Whitlam continued as leader of the Labor Party until 1977 and retired from politics in 1978. After that he taught at universities in Australia and overseas, and was Australia's representative to the United Nations Educational Scientific and Cultural Organisation (UNESCO) in Paris (1983-1989) as well as holding other international posts. He was always ready to give a pithy (and often erudite) quote—or even a two-hour lecture—about Australian politics and his own role as the great reforming Australian prime minister.

# CHAPTER 5

# 'LET ME MAKE MYSELF QUITE PLAIN'

## MALCOLM FRASER

Nine days after coming to office, Fraser appointed a committee to examine ways of reducing the size of the Commonwealth public service. The Administrative Review Committee headed by Henry Bland was appointed on 22 December 1975 and came to be known as the Razor Gang.

Fraser abolished or changed a number of Whitlam government reforms, and slashed the size of the public service and expenditure. But his government implemented many reforms, too. These included:

- establishing the Family Court of Australia
- establishing the television station SBS (Special Broadcasting Service) so that Australia's diverse cultures could have their own TV station broadcasting in many languages

- passing Aboriginal Land Rights laws
- banning whaling in Australian waters
- approving the building of a new Parliament House
- setting up the Australian Refugee Advisory Council to help the settlement of Vietnamese refugees in Australia.

## Malcolm Fraser

**Born in Melbourne in 1930, Malcolm Fraser came from a family of wealthy graziers. He studied at Oxford, graduated in 1952 and entered federal parliament at the age of 25 as Liberal Party member for Wannon. He was another tall, imposing politician, with a face that rarely showed emotion and made him seem hard-hearted instead of compassionate.**

**Whether consciously or not, he often prefaced his explanations to journalists with the phrase 'Let me make myself quite plain', as if to contrast his reserved personality with Whitlam's flamboyance.**

**Undoubtedly Fraser's best-remembered quote is, however, his statement to parliament that 'Life wasn't meant to be easy'. At the time many Australians were suffering from high interest rates and the high cost of petrol—and they didn't like a rich bloke who'd never had to struggle for money telling them that life was about hard work.**

But in fact the quote is from the Irish playwright, George Bernard Shaw, in 'Back to Methuselah' published in 1921. ""Life is not meant to be easy, my child; but take courage: it can be delightful." In an interview in 2004 Fraser was unable to remember whether he had given the full quote or not—but he said he certainly meant that life could be good, too, if you worked for it.

After leaving parliament Fraser remained politically active, frequently criticising Liberal Party policy—and even resigning from the party eventually in 2009. He was active in causes such as Aboriginal reconciliation and support for refugees, and in organisations such as Care International and the Australian Republican Movement.

Ironically, Fraser and Whitlam ended up as friends, both dedicated to an Australia without racial or religious prejudice, following its own path, not necessarily that of the United States, with equal opportunities for all.

Fraser was a strong critic of the apartheid regime in South Africa, where white people ruled a mostly black nation, and white minority rule in Rhodesia (now Zimbabwe). Some Whitlam supporters surprised themselves by acknowledging Fraser's stance against racism both around the world and at home.

He was a stern defender of the rights of Indigenous Australians, remembering with disgust that, many years ago, when he'd travelled with his father into the desert to photograph the scenery, he'd met a white hunter who boasted that he'd 'only got one'—not a kangaroo, but an Indigenous person. The Northern Territory Land Rights Act of 1976 allowed traditional owners to claim land that wasn't owned by anyone else. (The Northern Territory was under the control of the Commonwealth government until 1978.) The act also created a commission to hear claims. For the first time there was a legal way for Indigenous Australians to establish ownership of their land.

And Australia became an even more multicultural society under Fraser than it had been under Whitlam. From 1975 to 1982 about 200,000 migrants arrived from Asian countries, including nearly 56,000 Vietnamese people who applied as refugees, some arriving in small leaky boats. The newspapers now called refugees who arrived like this 'boat people'.

## 'Boat People'

The first refugees from the war in Vietnam arrived as 'boat people' in Darwin in 1976, the year the war ended. As well as Vietnamese, the refugees in their small battered fishing boats also included people from Cambodia and Laos. The trip was dangerous. Many drowned or died of hunger, thirst or sunstroke, while the elderly and babies died simply from the stress and terror of the voyage. Others were killed or taken by pirates.

From 1976 to 1981 about 56 boats came from Vietnam and some 2,100 'boat people' were granted entry to Australia. The Fraser government was worried about the numbers arriving, but was concerned about international criticism if it refused to admit the asylum seekers. The government also realised that this was a tiny proportion of Australia's annual immigration total.

Some Australians were afraid that their country would become too Asian. Others, whose ancestors had also found their way here in small leaky ships a century earlier across a vast and dangerous ocean, loved the new diversity—and the food. There was the old fear, too, that new arrivals would 'take our jobs'. Australia was subject to movements in the international economy and times were getting harder—but there wasn't much an Australian prime minister could do about it.

## CHAPTER 6

# NO MORE OIL?

It was called the 'oil crisis'. There'd been one in 1973, but in 1979 the Arab oil-producing states suddenly limited the amount of oil they were prepared to sell, and thereby pushed up the price. It looked like the age of cheap oil was over.

The prosperity of the western world was built on Arab oil wells. Our cars, freight trains and planes ran on oil: it was used to fire power stations and make a large range of plastics too, as well as for industry. Without oil food wouldn't get delivered, factories would stop production and workers would lose their jobs.

> **18 JANUARY 1977**
> **GRANVILLE DISASTER**
> 83 people died when a train from the Blue Mountains was derailed and crashed into a bridge over the line at Granville in Sydney.

Meanwhile, people queued at service stations to buy petrol before that week's supply at the pump ran out. Prices climbed higher and higher. Australia is a big country and most people had got used to driving a few hours to the coast, or to see friends, without really thinking much about the cost of the fuel it took to get there.

The fear was made worse by the predictions that the world was going to run out of oil, though no one was sure when. Oil mostly comes from the remains of algae and diatoms that once lived in vast shallow seas, and coal comes from ancient forests. Once the deposits had gone there'd be no more. With the economic power of Japan and the rapid industrialisation of China and India, the demand for oil was growing. How long would it last?

Australia had its own oil; so did the United States and some other countries, though none as massive as the deposits in the Middle East. Now oil companies scrambled to find new oil fields. The Australian government invested more in coal-fired power stations as Australia has vast reserves of black coal and—even more damaging to the environment—brown coal. Mining it seemed like a good idea at the time.

As the Arab nations released more oil onto the market, the crisis finished, though the price of oil would stay much higher than it had been before and would continue to grow steadily higher over the next two decades.

## A Taste of Terrorism

### 13 February 1979

Australia had its first taste of terrorism when a bomb hidden in a garbage bin exploded outside the Hilton Hotel in Sydney, where prime minister Malcolm Fraser and eleven other national leaders were staying, before a Commonwealth Heads of Government Meeting (CHOGM). Although the target was almost certainly the heads of government, the two garbage collectors who picked up the bin containing the bomb were killed instead. A policeman later died of his injuries and seven other people were badly injured.

Police blamed members of the Ananda Marga religious group, but no one was ever convicted, and no group ever claimed responsibility. Some said that the bomb had been planted by ASIO, to show that a national security agency was really needed; others blamed the police. The true bomber and the reason for the bombing remain a mystery.

## Good Ideas Go Bust

Few realised that the coal-fired power stations weren't just emitting toxic fumes nearby. They also released massive amounts of carbon dioxide ($CO_2$) that would help warm the Earth's atmosphere.

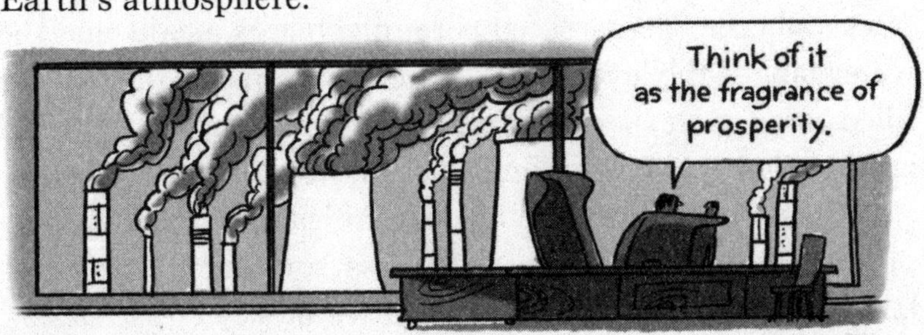

Other ideas that had seemed good at the time were creating massive problems, too. The Snowy Mountains Hydro-electric Scheme was killing the once great River Murray. Dead river red gums stood stark and white where there had once been great flood plains. Even worse, the water was growing saltier. Would it soon be too salty to use for the massive irrigation areas that supplied much of the fresh produce for Australia and the Pacific? Would the soil that the water was pumped onto become too salty to grow anything?

In the 19th century Australians had congratulated themselves on the vast cleared acres that turned 'unproductive' bush into farmland. But now the topsoil was blowing away. It took about six tonnes of topsoil to grow every tonne of wheat in Australia. Large areas were becoming too salty to grow crops—not just because of irrigation with slightly salty water, but because clearing the trees and other deep-rooted perennial plants meant that the water table—the level below which the pores in the soil are filled with water—rose higher. Suddenly, areas that had grown good grass for animals became almost like deserts.

A new word covered it all: desertification, turning once-productive land into desert. Unless something was done large parts of Australia's farmland would become useless.

So something was done—in fact, many somethings were done. Government programs began to identify areas that were in danger of becoming too salty, and gave advice on repairing the vast erosion gullies spreading across the paddocks. But most action was taken by the farmers themselves.

Within a decade most farmers in the vast Greening Australia movement went from cutting down trees to planting them, diverting water flows across paddocks so they no longer kept deepening the erosion gullies. Many even started to fence off marshes, creeks and rivers, to stop sheep and cattle from polluting them with manure. Not all farmers did this—and in many areas clearing continued. But there was a general concern for the land, a realisation that without care our wide brown land would lose its green.

## *El Nino*

The drought began in mid-1978—though it was many months before anyone realised that it wasn't raining anymore.

Non-Indigenous Australians were learning more about their country and for the first time were recognising that the great ocean currents around the continent affected the weather on land. The *El Nino* Southern Oscillation brought rain to South America, where the warm current was named after the Christ child, because it brought increased fishing for the Peruvian fishermen around Christmas time. But in Australia it brought brown hills, dry dams and starving animals along the east and south of the continent. Even though the rural areas suffered and the price of meat and vegies rose, Australians in the cities still had enough water to hose their green lawns and put a sprinkler on the rose bushes.

For now.

## The Death of Azaria Chamberlain

In August 1980, ten-week old Azaria Chamberlain vanished from her parents' tent at Uluru, then called Ayers Rock. Her mother, Lindy Chamberlain, claimed a dingo took her and the first inquest into Azaria's disappearance agreed; at the second inquest the police said that Azaria had been killed by her mother and that her father had helped hide the body. Lindy Chamberlain was convicted and sent to jail, but she and her husband were later exonerated and released after much of the evidence used against them was shown to be wrong. A third inquest delivered an open finding, which meant that the case was officially unsolved.

Reactions to the case brought together a range of prejudices: some anti-feminist, some anti-religious (Michael Chamberlain was a pastor in the Seventh Day Adventist Church, though early reports said it was a 'cult'), and some responses were anti-dingo. Australian opinion was divided. People claimed they were certain Lindy Chamberlain did it and others were equally sure it was the dingo. A movie starring Meryl Streep was made about the case, songs written and bad taste dingo jokes were told for years. Azaria's body has never been found, although six years after she disappeared her matinee jacket was discovered at the base of the Rock.

# CHAPTER 7

# THE BIG BOLD EIGHTIES

Fraser won two more federal elections—in 1977 and 1980. He was finally defeated by Australian Labor Party leader Bob Hawke in March 1983.

## BOB HAWKE

Hawke liked to think of himself as an old-fashioned Aussie larrikin, fond of a joke, he loved his sport, didn't mind a drink—though while he was still leader of the Australian Council of Trade Unions, he decided to aim for the prime ministership and gave up alcohol. He was a big bold prime minister for a big bold era.

**COMMONWEALTH V STATES**

**12 NOVEMBER 1981**
Malcolm Fraser declared the Great Barrier Reef a marine park—despite angry protests from Queensland's Bjelke-Petersen state government.

Robert James Lee Hawke was born in Bordertown, South Australia, the son of a Congregational minister and a school teacher. A graduate in law and arts from the University of Western Australia, he went to Oxford University as a Rhodes Scholar. He served as president of the ACTU from 1969 to 1980. With his shock of salt-and-pepper and later silver-grey hair, outgoing manner and raspy broad Australian accent, he was a well-known and popular figure, with a reputation for resolving trade union conflicts by using a consensus approach.

Hawke was elected to parliament in October 1980. Just over two years later, opposition leader Bill Hayden resigned, and Hawke became leader of the ALP, on the same day that Fraser called the election—unaware that he would be fighting not Hayden but Hawke. By then Fraser was so unpopular that Hayden said when Hawke took his job, 'A drover's dog could lead Labor to victory at the present time.'

Hawke led his party to the greatest federal Labor victory since 1943, gaining 75 of the 125 seats in the House of Representatives and 30 of the 60 Senate seats. He would be in office for eight years and become Australia's longest-serving Labor prime minister.

The new Hawke Labor government was much more cautious than the dynamic Whitlam government and Hawke was seen as moving Labor to the right. A month after his election Hawke called a meeting of leaders of business, government and trade unions to try to bring them all together and form what he called the Accord. It was an attempt to find consensus about economic and industrial relations. Instead of announcing strikes and lock-outs, everyone would sit down and try to come to agreement. It was very much a development of Hawke's former role as trade union leader. He cultivated close contacts with business—not always without controversy—and an agreement with the trade unions that discouraged strikes.

Most of the Whitlam programs that had cost a lot of money—such as free health care and tertiary education for everyone—were gradually cut back in the next decade. In February 1984 Hawke replaced Medibank (which had been partially dismantled by the Fraser government) with Medicare. This was financed with a levy on incomes above a certain level.

**Ash Wednesday**
**February, 1983**
**Extreme bushfires raged across much of Victoria and South Australia. They killed 75 people, injured about 2,676, destroyed 2,500 buildings and damaged many more.**

Hawke also wound back Whitlam's vision of free university places and introduced a Higher Education Contribution Scheme (HECS), by which students paid subsidised fees for university subjects either up-front or on graduation, once they were earning an income above a specified level. But the laws about divorce, anti-discrimination legislation, Indigenous rights, equality for women, the feeling that we were proud of our own culture, our own history as a land of people from many places, not just the UK, and the sense that we were part of Asia and the Pacfic remained.

## Landmark Dates in Australian History

**On 26 October 1985 Ayers Rock was given back to its traditional owners, the Pitjantjatjara and Yankunytjatjara people, and on 15 December 1993 its name became Ayers Rock/Uluru under the dual naming policy—and reversed to Uluru/Ayers Rock on 6 November 2002. The Pitjantjatjara lease it back to the Commonwealth to be run as a national park, but access by tourists is controlled by the Anangu (traditional owners).**

**On 29 March 1984 Charles Perkins became the first Indigenous person to head a Commonwealth department. He was appointed Secretary of the Department of Aboriginal Affairs.**

The Hawke government made economic reform one of its most important goals. Once the UK joined the European Economic Community in 1972, Australia realised it could no longer rely on the sell-it-all-to-Britain approach. We were part of the global economy. Hawke scrapped many tariffs—taxes that were added to imported goods so that home-manufactured goods would be cheaper and therefore protect Australian industries. But by 1992, 11 per cent of Australians were unemployed. It was the highest level since the Great Depression of the 1930s.

Many of Australia's companies were bought by giant multinational corporations. Economists and politicians encouraged the principle of 'globalisation', by which the world was seen as having one giant interconnected economy. Making money was the main aim and people who made a lot of money, like property developer Alan Bond (who would later spend time in jail for fraud) were the heroes of the decade. By 1987, the character of Gordon Gekko in the Oscar-winning film 'Wall Street' was meant to be the object of satire for his slogan 'Greed is Good', but some people still didn't see the irony.

## Big Business, Big Hair

The 80s glittered. The idealism of the 60s and 70s gave way to 'If you've got it, flaunt it'. Newspapers began to feature the ever more flamboyant antics of people who were famous just for being rich. The bright colours and flowing clothes of the 70s gave way to 'power dressing', with dark business suits and padded shoulders for women, as though they were showing that they were exactly the right shape for the male business world. Women's hair went BIG—fluffed out like a lion's mane as though to show they could be just as ferocious. Men's hair grew tidy again, with many of the beards and nearly all the sideburns shaved off. Older men who were going bald or blokes who wanted to look tough had severe haircuts that shaved off nearly all their hair—a fashion that would stay around for at least another 30 years.

Businesspeople often started the day with a breakfast meeting, or 'power breakfast', and spent more time with their work colleagues than their families. They went to expensive conferences, self-improvement seminars and spent huge sums on gym memberships.

But there was glitter, too: lots of big jewellery, even sparkling eye shadow or bright colours for your hair. Parties were BIG. In the past Australian kids might have had a

backyard birthday party, if they were lucky, and a big shindig when they turned 21. Now even families who weren't rich put on big parties at clubs or restaurants when kids turned 18, as well as 21. Even toddlers had birthday parties at McDonalds or one of the new 'party centres' where you might ride mini-bikes or bounce on jumping castles. And when you left school, hundreds of dollars would be spent on a 'formal'. Groups of kids might hire a limo or horse and carriage to get there. It was a long way from a bit of coloured cellophane over the lights at the old school social.

Most families had more money in the 80s to spend on stuff, too—though they probably didn't realise it, because people's expectations were higher. For the past 200 years most Australians had bought essentials, unless they were rich. But now even average families had two cars, or maybe three if the kids were old enough to drive. They had at least two TV sets and gadgets that they hardly ever used, like crepe-makers and ice-cream machines: appliances that were expensive, had a single function and weren't a bit versatile.

Toys were cheap and mostly made of plastic. They didn't last long—the plastic cracked in the sun. But they didn't need to last, because everyone wanted something new. In the past things like metal tricycles and wooden swings were handed down from parents to kids and even to their grandkids. Now kids had cupboards full of toys and threw them away when they got tired of them, except for a select few they really loved. Like the appliances, toys were cheap, because they were made by workers in countries such as China, India or the Philippines, on wages that often didn't pay enough to allow them to eat properly. This was one of the ugly sides of the glamour associated with globalisation.

Australian houses were changing, too. The houses of the 20s and 30s had been small cottages on big blocks of land, so you could grow a big vegie garden and lots of fruit trees down the back, with a shed to do household repairs in, big enough for a car—if you were one of the lucky few owners—or to make a boat in. Your house would have two bedrooms and often a tiny bathroom and laundry, almost like an afterthought tacked on at the back. Many still had outdoor dunnies. The houses of the 50s had three bedrooms, a kitchen, a dining room and a living room.

But now in the 70s and 80s, the houses were big and the blocks of land were small. True, land for building close to the main capital cities was harder to find, but the small size of the blocks was mostly due to the developers' eye for a profit. The journalist Craig McGregor later observed that the quarter-acre block Australians traditionally dreamt of had been replaced by the quarter-acre house. Now there was almost no garden.

Most houses had four bedrooms, two bathrooms and the rumpus room had become a 'family room' with the kitchen off it. Formal dining rooms were rare now—unless you were posh. Even though women still did most of the cooking, a lot of men cooked now, too—and no one wanted to be shut off in the kitchen from what the rest of the family were doing.

The tiny backyards didn't seem to matter much. The kids of the 80s had their favourite TV shows, instead of their favourite outdoor games like cowboys and Indians, or making cubby houses. You weren't even stuck with what was on the three or four TV channels, either—if they were showing boring programs you could hire a video from the new video stores that were popping up in every suburb and town.

Going to the pictures had been the weekly treat for many Australians ever since the 1920s. TV had cut into the audiences a bit, and now most cinemas, drive-ins and theatres had shut down. Why spend the money and time getting to a theatre when you could wait six months for it come 'come out on video' and see it at home more comfortably and much cheaper? The video was just one of the inventions that were changing the way we relaxed and worked.

Hawke may not have been a visionary prime minister. But the way Australians lived and worked changed dramatically while he was in office. And a lot of the changes were due to material wealth and new gadgets.

## Our New Best Friends

The most important of these was the personal computer.

It's hard to say what was the world's first computer—calculating machines of some sort had been around for centuries, or even thousands of years. But Australia's first digital computer, the CSIR Mk 1, which stood taller than a human being and occupied a couple of metres of wall space, was in use in 1949 at the Council for Scientific and Industrial Research, the precursor to CSIRO.

Back in the 50s sci-fi writers wrote stories about the time when one giant computer would rule the world. No one, it seemed, predicted what would really happen—that computers would get smaller, as well as much more powerful, so that they could fit on your desk, then your lap, and eventually in the palm of your hand.

Personal desktop computers went on sale in Australia in the late 1970s. But it wasn't till the mid-1980s that computers—still large clunky machines by today's standards—were starting to be used a lot in the workplace.

By the early 1990s most professional people used computers. Learning to adapt was hard for a lot of older people, especially men. Girls had often been taught typing at school, so they could work as secretaries—or assistants to businessmen and officials—typing up their handwritten letters, or taking dictation in shorthand and then typing the documents up for them. Now blokes had to do the typing themselves—and work out how to do it. (Many older people would always be two-finger or hunt-and-peck typists: reasonably quick, but still having to look at the keyboard instead of the screen as they worked.)

The profession of secretary just about vanished. In its place 'personal assistants' did all sorts of work, but that didn't include turning longhand writing into type or taking down dictation. Who wanted to wait for someone else to answer an email?

It was in the 1990s that the word 'email' began to be heard around the world, as slowly the individual personal computers were connected to the internet, at first down telephone lines, but then in the next decade, by satellite and radio waves.

Many people and places claim to have invented the internet. It may really have begun in the United States in the late 1960s, when the US Department of Defense wanted an emergency communication system. They linked computers over telephone lines so that if one computer failed to work, the others could still communicate with each other. The system was made more sophisticated by the American and Australian technicians working on the space program to send astronauts to the moon.

In the early 70s the @ sign was first used to separate the name of the user and their computer's name. By the end of the decade there were international computer networks for government projects and some businesses. In 1981 Australia connected to the Advanced Research Projects Agency Network (ARPANet), which opened the network up for commercial interest four years later. Then the university system AARNet(1) was connected in the late 80s. In 1989 Australia's first public internet service provider started up and the internet really took off! By the mid-90s most businesses and most kids were using the internet and email. Ten years later even their great grandparents would be using it.

But other gizmos changed our lives, too—such as mobile phones. In the 1950s only well-off households had a phone. If you lived in the suburbs and didn't have one, it wasn't far to walk to a red public phone box, where there was a phone you could use by putting coins into a slot—although lots of kids discovered that if you had no money you could dial the number, yell into the earpiece and the person on the other end of the line could hear you very faintly.

By the 1980s just about every home had a phone line connected to it. If you wanted to communicate as you moved around you needed a two-way radio: the kind used by police and emergency services. Australia's first mobile phones were launched in 1981 by Telecom (later Telstra). They were big clunky-looking black things and weighed more than half a kilo. They were expensive to buy and even more expensive to use. It was a real status symbol to pull your mobile phone out of your briefcase or handbag.

Slowly, however, mobiles became smaller, lighter and cheaper. But still in 1994 only about 4 per cent of Australians had a mobile phone. Ten years later more than 70 per cent would have one. Many of those would decide they now didn't need a landline phone in their homes, and lots of public phone boxes were demolished. Mobiles had become so tiny that you could carry them everywhere—and you needed to.

The old 9 to 5 working hours had changed, so you were never sure when you could catch someone on the phone, part-time and freelance workers needed to be available if a prospective employer called with a job, and people were on the move constantly after work hours, in their cars, out jogging or eating in restaurants. Having a mobile phone also became associated with personal security.

# Family Life?

Australian family life changed in the 80s, too. Most mums worked outside the home now, even if only part-time. Email and the internet also made it possible for parents to work from home occasionally. Homes now had big fridges, microwave ovens to heat up take-away or frozen food, bought ready-made at the supermarket or take-away shop or even delivered to your door.

All these new gadgets should have meant that everyone had more time to play and spend together. But it didn't work like that. The big houses meant that mortgages were bigger, so both parents had to work long hours to pay for them. Cities were getting bigger and roads even more crowded and there had been no real increase in government spending on public transport to cater for the growing population. More and more time was spent just getting from one place to another, or finding a spot to park the car. The days when most dads walked home from work, or had a 20-minute bus, train or tram ride were over.

Even free time was more regulated. There were after-school programs for kids, if both their parents were working; but there was lots of other organised stuff, too. In the past sporty kids might go to training one afternoon a week and play on Saturday, but now everyone seemed to have their free time taken up with swimming, music, dance lessons or maths coaching. And kids from a non-English speaking background were often sent to Saturday schools to keep up their family's first-language heritage. These were all things kids had learnt from friends and relatives a few decades earlier. Now they were taught professionally and parents drove their kids across town from one activity to the next—so they felt that they didn't have any spare time either.

Even at home, spare time was often organised around what was on TV. In many homes the TV was on all the time from breakfast till lights out. TV was no longer a novelty, but families still ate meals in front of it, just as they had when the first TV dinners were packaged in foil trays back in the 50s. There were no quiet spaces for long family conversations or games.

Most of the kids' games of a few decades earlier, like French cricket, hopscotch and marbles, had died out. Kids had more exciting things to do, like playing video games, sometimes competing with other kids, but mostly against the computer. Small backyards didn't just mean goodbye to the chook run and the vegie patch. There wasn't room to play outside either, and there was too much traffic on the roads for kids to play tennis or cricket in the street, as they had in the 50s.

# A Stir-fry and Sara Lee for Dinner

Sometime between 1970 and 1990, Australians developed their own unique way of eating.

It took in parts of most of the nation's cultures. A family might have stir-fry vegies or pasta, or a salad seasoned with Thai herbs and served with chips. Recipes came from newspapers and magazines rather than Mum or Grandma. And a lot more food came already prepared.

Supermarkets sold tubs of salad, packets of pre-cut vegies or mixed salad leaves and even tubs of mashed potato and pumpkin. The meat shelves came with kebabs that had already been marinated. Even people who cooked a lot would add tinned tomatoes instead of skinning and chopping their own, frozen peas, garlic paste or seasoning from a packet.

Food was a lot more fun. Instead of the Vegemite, peanut butter or jam sandwiches of the 50s, kids had salad wraps, sushi, rice paper rolls, paninos, blueberry muffins—food taken from many cultures and changed a bit to suit Australian tastes and ingredients. Christmas dinner might be turkey or salmon or sausages on the barbecue, with salads and dips from the supermarket, old English steamed pudding served with ice-cream instead of custard sauce, and panforte instead of mince pies.

In high-class restaurants it was called 'fusion food'—European ingredients using Asian cooking techniques and seasonings. Food tastes were changing in most places around the world, but finally after 200 years Australians had a cuisine that was not quite the same as anyone else's.

## Let's All Face the Music!

Ever since most Australian households had got record players and radios in the 1920s and 30s, parents had been yelling at their kids, 'Turn it down!'

Record players were out of date now—most music was heard on cassette tapes, which you could copy for your friends. (This was against the law, as it meant that the music makers didn't get any money from their work, but it happened a lot.) Young people still played their music much louder than their parents wanted, though.

Then on 1 July 1979 Sony released a thing called a Walkman—a pocket-sized machine that played music you could listen to through small earphones. By the early 80s lots of people were using one—or a cheaper copy. Kids could finally listen to their own music without adults complaining.

## Don't You Worry about That

For 21 years, Premier Joh Bjelke-Petersen led Queensland's conservative government. Bjelke-Petersen's government was arguably the most corrupt Australia has ever had, but the colourful premier with his wisecrack of 'Don't you worry about that' was still voted in at each election—with the help a gerrymander that meant some electorates could vote in a member of parliament with fewer than half the votes required in another electorate.

In early 1987 some of his supporters mounted a 'Joh for PM' campaign, to send him to Canberra. When his own party, the Nationals, finally dumped him as premier in late 1987, he insisted that he wouldn't leave and tried to recall parliament to vote him back in.

They didn't.

## Gap Years

Although the word 'gap year' didn't come into widespread use for another ten years or so, the idea of a year between school and uni probably started when Hawke changed the rules about living allowances at uni. If you'd supported yourself for a year you could get a living allowance. Otherwise, unless your parents or guardians were very badly off indeed, you either had to live at home (impossible for most country kids and for many city kids, who lived far away from a uni, too), go to uni part-time, or not at all.

And if you had to support yourself for a year, it was more fun to do it somewhere exotic. Fares to Europe and Asia were cheaper now than they had ever been. Kids backpacked around the world, working in bars, as nannies or as assistants in schools, sometimes in organised exchange schemes, but often just moving from place to place, perhaps with a mob of friends from school, or new friends they'd made on the way.

From the 80s to the 90s and the 2000s, more and more young Australians found jobs in Europe, either full-time or going from casual job to casual job to finance their travel. Some headed for the Oktoberfest beer festival in Germany. Others wanted to show they could get out of the way of a bull at Pamplona's Running of the Bulls in Spain. Many would find their way to Anzac Cove on Anzac Day, learning and inventing their past as they stood with many thousands of others at what was becoming a major pilgrimage destination for Australians.

And then they came home. It was a long way from the days when a sentence of transportation to Australia meant you were probably here for life. The world was growing smaller—or maybe we were just looking beyond our own backyard.

# We Want You to Like Us!

One of the greatest changes in the Hawke years was one that most Australians didn't see. Until Hawke, Labor party policy was decided by the rank-and-file members of the Labor party—Australians from all over the country, who voted for what the policies should be. But there was no rule that said the party leader had to follow the policies the members decide on. They usually did, though. The great visions of the Whitlam years were the result of many, many committees of experts, academics and concerned people who had worked out how something as big as Medibank, for example, could be put into place.

Bob Hawke was a man who loved to be loved. He also wanted to win elections. And there was a growing industry in public relations, with spin doctors and focus groups run by researchers, who could work out what the public wanted and then spin public opinion to make people believe that a product was good to buy—or that a government policy was a good thing.

**Party Time**

**26 JANUARY 1988**
Australia celebrated the Bicentenary: 200 years since the landing of the First Fleet. But many Indigenous and other Australians were angry at celebrating what they said had been an invasion of someone else's country.

**9 MAY 1988**
The Queen opened the new parliament house in Canberra. It was bigger, grander and more modern than the old one further down the hill.

Increasingly Hawke and his ministers—not the Labor Party membership itself—decided what his government should do. When Hawke got up to give his speech before the 1987 election, he made a promise that rang around Australia—that by 1990 no Australian child would live in poverty.

It sounded wonderful. But in fact it was an impulsive, last-minute addition with no real thought and certainly no economic planning behind it. And of course it didn't happen. It was a meaningless 'motherhood' statement—empty words that sounded good and that everyone would agree with.

Hawke didn't invent the concept of political spin—and he wasn't the first to use it, either. But it was in his time as prime minister that policies increasingly became determined by public opinion polls and public relations people played increasingly important roles in making the public think what the government wanted them to.

And another invisible influence crept up on us, too.

## The Hole in the Ozone Layer

Every period in history seems to have its threat. In the 1980s the world, and Australians, discovered that an invisible part of the atmosphere, the ozone layer that protected the world from too much deadly ultraviolet light—was vanishing.

It was catastrophic news for the whole world. Too much UV wouldn't just kill humans—it would kill animals, plants and change the world beyond recognition. And this might come even sooner for Australia, because it was located in the southern hemisphere, where the layer was thinnest—so thin it was called a 'hole' over Antarctica and in summer the hole travelled up across Australia.

And humans were to blame.

The thinning ozone levels were caused mostly by the chlorofluorocarbons (CFCs) released into the atmosphere from fridges, air-conditioning units and fire extinguishers, though there were other causes, too. Chlorofluorocarbons were first created in 1928 as non-toxic, non-flammable refrigerants. By 1985, ozone levels in the Antarctic were 10 per cent less than they should have been—and that situation was going to get much worse.

This was the first time the world had really faced a problem that affected us all—more comprehensively than either of the so-called world wars. In 1985 in Vienna and 1987 in Montreal world leaders gathered together to work out treaties which would commit signatories to limiting or banning substances that might destroy the ozone layer.

Not all countries agreed—and even if they had, it might not have been enough.

In the past, governments—or kings or other rulers—could pretty much control what happened, but since World War II the world's biggest companies had become what were known as 'multinational corporations'—companies that were so big they didn't really belong to any one country. Nor were they answerable at law for their actions in the same way that earlier companies had been. If one country's government tried to limit them, the offending corporation could move their headquarters somewhere else. But in 1991 the multinational company Du Pont agreed to stop making CFCs. By 1996 there were no CFCs being made in the US or Europe.

CFCs are still being made and used—but in much smaller amounts, because cheaper and better alternatives for fridges and air-conditioning units have been invented. And since 2000 the ozone hole is slowly—and unevenly—getting smaller. By 2050, at this rate, the hole will have vanished and the protective ozone layer will have been restored.

It's easier to fight an enemy you can see than a complicated problem like the hole in the ozone layer. But countries had got together to solve the problem. And it seems to have worked.

## CHAPTER 8

# OUR CHANGING NATION

Whitlam, Fraser and, to a lesser extent, Hawke had tried to improve the lives of Indigenous Australians. But although many Indigenous people were now achieving success, for many others things were getting worse, instead of better.

In cities this was often because Indigenous people lived in cheap neighbourhoods—and those were the ones that attracted people with drug, alcohol and other problems. It was all too easy for young Indigenous people to be sucked into these dangerous cultures.

In more remote areas the things townspeople took for granted—clean running water, indoor bathrooms, hospitals, schools, programs to help you stop drinking, sports facilities or cinemas—simply didn't exist. Houses were often crammed with several families or one giant extended family of many aunties and uncles, grandparents, teenagers, toddlers and infants trying to live in one house, just because there weren't enough houses for them all.

How had this happened, when so many good people had been trying to make a difference?

Partly it was because the money often went to the state governments rather than directly to the Indigenous communities, and it wasn't even used for their benefit. Partly it was because the enormous budgets of the government departments spent a lot more money on bureaucrats, committees or administrators than on houses and schools for Indigenous people. Overwhelming problems had also developed in some communities that were already hobbled by disadvantage and dysfunction and ripped apart by rivalries and hostility.

Mostly, though, it was because there was still a massive double standard. White kids living in remote areas got School of the Air and correspondence lessons, government boarding schools and help with governesses and live-in programs. But Indigenous kids were often left out of this support system altogether.

White families had the Flying Doctor and rural hospitals, but many Indigenous communities didn't even have a nurse—often because proper housing and support wasn't provided for them. It wasn't just help the Indigenous communities needed—it was a different way of thinking, an assumption that if white kids in remote regions got schools and medical care, even if it cost the taxpayer a lot to fund, then black kids were entitled to these services, too.

And there was another, much deeper problem. Many Indigenous communities were established on land where their ancestors had lived for generations—or had been part of nations that had lasted for thousands, even tens of thousands of years. But, legally, they didn't own that land. The land belonged to the federal or state governments. Other people could borrow money from a bank to build a house and pay it back gradually. But you couldn't do that if the land wasn't legally yours—especially if you didn't have a well-paid job or the education to get one in the first place.

## Eddie Mabo Makes it Happen

Eddie Mabo

For the previous ten years a group of people from the Torres Strait had been fighting to change the land rights situation, led by an extraordinary man called Eddie Mabo.

Eddie Koiki Mabo was born on Mer, or Murray Island, in 1936, at a time when it was almost impossible for an Indigenous Australian to get a good education or a good job. His mother died in childbirth, so his Uncle Benny Mabo and Aunt Maiga adopted him under customary law. They also taught him about his people's land.

But at 17 he was exiled from Mer for bad behaviour—just a prank, but in those days anyone deemed a troublemaker was quickly shipped off the islands. He worked on pearling boats and then as a railway worker in Townsville, where he became a union representative. In 1967 he began work as a gardener at James Cook University. His time on the campus was immensely important as he sat in on lectures, went to the library and read anthropological studies of his people.

While talking with Eddie in 1974, a couple of academics realised that he believed that he and his people owned their land, so they told him that in fact it was owned by the Crown. His ideas of justice and his devotion to his childhood nation began to crystallise.

In 1967, Eddie Mabo helped organise a seminar called 'We the Australians'. Even though he was still officially a gardener, he also gave lectures on Torres Strait culture and Indigenous politics. In 1972 he and his wife and family tried to go back to Mer to visit his uncle, who was dying. They got as far as Thursday Island, then were turned back. Eddie Mabo was still seen as a troublemaker—but worse: a political one. His uncle died without ever seeing his adopted son again or meeting his grandchildren.

Eddie Mabo was angry. In 1981 there was a land rights conference held at the university at which he gave a speech that defined land ownership and inheritance on Mer. A lawyer in the audience suggested that there should be a test case before the High Court to claim land rights through the court system.

The Murray Islanders decided that they would challenge the legal principle of 'terra nullius' and that Eddie Mabo would lead the case, with a team including Am Passi, Father Dave Passi, James Rice and Celuia Mapo Salee.

In 1982 Eddie Mabo went to the High Court of Australia and declared his people's rights to their land. The first decision was that, as Eddie Koiki Mabo was not Bennie Mabo's son, he had no right to inherit Mabo land. This was immensely upsetting to him, but the finding was appealed. The case took ten years to hear. Eddie Mabo kept fighting, but he knew he was dying, too. He died from cancer on 21 January 1992, aged 56.

**DEATHS IN CUSTODY**

**15 APRIL 1991**
**The Royal Commission into Aboriginal Deaths in Custody released its final report. The commission investigated the deaths of 99 Aboriginal prisoners between 1980 and 1989. Its report comprised eleven volumes and more than 5,000 pages and included 339 recommendations.**

Five months later, on 3 June 1992, the High Court delivered a 6 to 1 verdict in favour of Mabo in the case of Mabo v State of Queensland. The 200-year-old idea of terra nullius—that white settlers had come to an unowned land—had been overturned. While the court did say that since that time many Indigenous rights had been extinguished, it ruled that those nations which could show unbroken ties to their land owned it.

Eddie Mabo had won.

He was buried in Townsville, but his grave was vandalised with Nazi swastikas and racist graffiti, and the carving of his face was stolen. His family removed his headstone and decided to bury him again on Mer.

At last Eddie had come home.

On the following Australia Day Eddie Mabo was named Father of the Year, not just as father to his own ten children, but to all of those Indigenous people who had fought for the right to own their land. On 21 May 2008, James Cook University named its Townsville campus library, where Eddie Mabo in his years as a gardener had read and taught himself so much about the history of his people, the Eddie Koiki Mabo Library.

Eddie Mabo's struggle led to the Native Title Act in 1993, which enabled Indigenous people throughout Australia to claim traditional rights to unalienated land.

Three years later in 1996, the Wik people of Cape York and the Thayorre people of Queensland tested native title further through the courts. The court held that native title rights could co-exist alongside the rights of pastoralists who owned cattle and sheep stations. When pastoralists and Aboriginal rights were in conflict, the pastoralists' rights would prevail. Graziers could continue to run their cattle or sheep and build fences and dig dams, but the Indigenous people were to have access to the land, as well. The image of Wik elder Gladys Tybingoompa doing a victory dance outside the High Court and Parliament House is etched in the memories of a generation.

Many white Australians rejoiced at the Mabo case; in a bitter irony, others were scared that the idea of 'native title' would spread and that their homes or parks would be stolen from them by Indigenous claims.

## Chapter 9

# Paul Keating and the Recession We Had to Have

In December 1991 Hawke was deposed as Labor Party leader, and prime minister, by Paul Keating, just as Bill Hayden had earlier been deposed by Hawke. The public had grown tired of Hawke. Some said his celebrated charisma had leaked away. Others felt that he had far too cosy a relationship with big business. His popularity wasn't helped by claims from Keating, who was his treasurer and deputy, that Hawke had promised to resign in his favour—then changed his mind. Also Australians had been in recession for two years, with high unemployment and rising interest rates.

> **Earthquake!**
>
> **29 December 1989**
>
> **Newcastle, NSW was hit by an earthquake measuring 5.6 on the Richter scale. It killed 13 people and caused more than $1.5 billion damage, partly because the building codes allowed unsafe buildings to be put up.**

Interest rates went up to nearly 16 per cent—in other words, if you had borrowed $100,000 to buy your house, you had to pay more than $16,000 each year in interest payments. Many people were forced to sell their homes and house prices dropped by nearly a third.

The value of the dollar dropped, too, so that foreign manufactured cars, videos, TV sets and other imported goods were much more expensive to buy. At one time Australia had produced its own radios, ships and most other goods. But now, every year, more Australian manufacturers, shipyards and businesses either went bust or went overseas, were sold to a multinational company or became multinationals themselves.

Treasurer Paul Keating called it 'the recession we had to have', saying it wasn't his fault—nations across the world were in recession, too, many far worse off than Australia. He also believed that Australia had become so uncompetitive by hiding behind tariff walls and restrictive banking arrangements that we had to reorganise our economy drastically, so that we could compete with the rest of the world. If Australia didn't change, he said, we would become a 'banana republic', one of the poorest nations and a bit of a joke.

Most Australians had no idea what Keating was talking about. They saw only the jobs that had been lost, the rising prices, and the high interest rates.

Hawke's popularity had also taken a hit when he sent Australian troops to support the US invasion of Iraq in 1991, after the Iraqi dictator Saddam Hussein invaded the neighbouring country of Kuwait. The UK, Saudi Arabia and Egypt also sent forces to what would be known as the First Gulf War, with its final confrontation Operation Desert Storm.

Kuwait, like Iraq, was oil-rich. Many, or even most, Australians saw the war as a US attempt to get control of the oil fields and to help maintain stability in nearby Saudi Arabia (again to make sure the people of the United States could get the oil they needed. Australia, too, of course, depended on much the same oil supply). When the peace agreement was signed, keeping Iraq out of Kuwait but keeping the dictator Saddam Hussein in power, others felt that the armed forces should have kept going to Baghdad to depose him, even though the UN mandate was only for the liberation of Kuwait. The whole affair damaged Hawke's reputation even further.

At the time, Hawke was the only Labor prime minister to have been removed from office by his own party. Treasurer Paul Keating, who had been responsible for many of the economic reforms under Hawke, took over as prime minister. Two months later Hawke resigned from his seat in the House of Representatives.

## BANKSTOWN BOY

Paul Keating was born in the working class western Sydney suburb of Bankstown in 1944. He left school at 14 and in 1969, at the age of 25, entered federal parliament as the Labor member for Blaxland. He dressed smartly, had a passion for antiques and Mahler, and had a sharp debating wit—often too sharp for the electorate.

Like Whitlam, Keating had a vision, but a very different one. Keating's centred on his economic reforms, though he too was committed to Indigenous rights, a republican Australia and closer trade and cultural ties with Asia.

Paul Keating won the March 1993 election for Labor in his own right. He described it as 'the sweetest victory of all' because many had expected him to lose. But the economy was still in a bad way—unemployment was now at 11.4 per cent.

Keating tried to create new jobs: in 1992 he released the One Nation statement, committing the government to tax cuts as a strategy for economic recovery. The Australian National Training Authority Act 1992 was aimed at reforming vocational education and training. It also gave a wage to young people training for jobs. The Disability Discrimination Act 1992 meant that employers could no longer discriminate against people with a disability. If they could do the job as well as other applicants, then they should get it.

In 1994 Keating released a white paper called Working Nation: a $6.5 billion plan to bring unemployment down to 5 per cent at the turn of the century by addressing youth unemployment, training strategies and increasing workforce skills across the country. He also launched Creative Nation, a cultural policy linking government support for the arts with future economic prosperity.

Keating continued the Labor tradition of emphasising relations within the Asia-Pacific region. His first overseas trip as prime minister was to Indonesia in April 1992 and his government moved to strengthen Australian links with the Association of South-East Asian Nations (ASEAN) and the Asia-Pacific Economic Co-operation (APEC) forum.

This growing closeness with Indonesia worried many Australians, too. In February 1992, Indonesia had cracked down heavily on protesters in East Timor's capital Dili, when they called for free elections. But Keating wanted a free trade organisation of Asia-Pacific countries. In April 1992, he met Indonesia's President Suharto, seeking his support for turning the APEC into a body that would guide the overall development of free trade and practical economic cooperation in the region.

In 1993 Keating's dream seemed to be coming true, when US President Clinton hosted an APEC meeting in Seattle. But Malaysia's President Mahathir, who regarded Australia as a white colonial nation rather than a truly Asian one, refused to attend.

Australia chaired the South Pacific Forum in 1995 when France announced a new round of nuclear testing in the Pacific. Objecting to the tests Keating wrote, 'the Pacific Ocean is our Europe'.

He believed that by lowering tariff levels within the Asia-Pacific region, deregulating the banking and finance sectors and tying Australia to the economic strength of China, Japan and the United States, he could bring Australia out of recession. But many, even in his own party, thought he should be doing more to protect Australian jobs, rather than letting Australians buy cheap goods from overseas.

Keating was also a dedicated republican. He wanted to have an Australian as the head of state instead of the Queen or governor-general, partly to make Australia look like its own nation, instead of a remnant of European colonialism. In April 1993, he appointed a Republic Advisory Committee to come up with ways for Australia to become a republic. Who would choose the head of state? And what powers would that person have? Would the head of state be merely someone to attend public functions and make speeches that didn't say much, but said it well? Or would there be real powers—like those exercised by the governor-general when he dismissed the Whitlam government?

In 1992 Keating had given a ground-breaking and now famous speech at Redfern Park to a largely Indigenous audience on the subject of Aboriginal reconciliation and was the first prime minister to acknowledge responsibility for the ongoing difficulties faced by Indigenous Australians. 'We committed the murders. We took the children from their mothers. We practised discrimination and exclusion. It was our ignorance and our prejudice.'

It was Keating who introduced the laws that Eddie Mabo and others had battled so long for. The Native Title legislation became law in 1993, giving Indigenous people throughout

Australia the right to claim traditional rights to 'unalienated' land—land that hadn't been bought or leased by other people. It was followed by the Land Fund Act 1994.

Regardless of his vision for Australia, Keating simply wasn't popular. Cartoon and newspaper articles portrayed him as arrogant: knowing that he was clever and showing it. He didn't seem sympathetic to the problems of ordinary people. There were various scandals, too, with ministers Graham Richardson, Ros Kelly and Carmen Lawrence accused of acting improperly. And some commentators said that the Australian public had become tired of constant change.

Unemployment was down—a bit—to 9 per cent, and interest rates were lower than in the early 90s. But foreign debt was growing. Almost every day there seemed to be a news item about another factory that had gone broke, with jobs lost, or another Australian company bought by an overseas firm—with the jobs going offshore.

Liberal Party leader John Howard promised to cut government spending and to be a wise and cautious leader in tough economic times. In the March 1996 election he led the Liberal-National Party coalition to an overwhelming 40-seat majority in the House of Representatives.

## Chapter 10

# Hair Gel, Goths and Credit Cards

Australians were comfortable—well, most Australians—and by and large they didn't want to think about those who weren't. Even the 'mortgage crisis' mostly meant that the families affected weren't able to have the luxuries they had grown used to: eating out, legs of roast lamb and the latest model TV sets. During the 1990s the average income of Australians almost doubled.

Australians were no longer a nation of sportsmen and women. We watched sport on TV instead, or went to outdoor venues only to watch big interstate or international matches. At one time families had gathered to sing songs around the piano. Now kids listened to pop music by international stars like Michael Jackson, which was heard all around the world.

International brand names were important, too. Tennis or sandshoes had become 'sneakers' and then 'joggers' or 'trainers'—with fashionable brand names like Reebok or Adidas costing over $100, about the same amount as a week's old age pension. People were even held up by thieves for their Reeboks. The highly paid advertisers had done their job. An international sports star such as US basketball player Michael Jordan or Magic Johnson would become the face of a branded product, made for a few cents by kids in third world countries, and sold to westerners for vast amounts.

Tough was in fashion—odd, considering that John Howard said he wanted a kinder, gentler Australia. Goths wore nothing but black, with black mascara around their eyes and often white make-up and red lips to make them look like vampires. Black was fashionable for everyone, the colour for women and for men, too. It was incidentally practical—cities had become more polluted and white clothes could look grimy around the collar from sweat or make-up after a long day.

Once tattoos had only been for big tough men such as bikies or sailors, to show they could stand the pain. Now even young girls had tattoos of butterflies or birds on their backs or ankles. And some of their older sisters had a great deal more.

Many parents yelled 'No!' at the very idea of their kids getting a tattoo. Tattoos were for life, unless you wanted laser surgery that might scar you for life instead. But piercings would at least grow over if you changed your mind later and hair would always grow out if you felt you'd made a mistake. Women had had the lobes of their ears pierced for thousands of years so they could wear earrings that wouldn't slip off. But now ears could have two, three or even a dozen piercings, with studs all along the lobe. Some parents worried that their kids' ears would end up like lace and there were stories about earlobes falling off through too many piercings. Noses were pierced, navels were pierced, tongues (and other, even more sensitive, parts) were pierced.

A much bigger range of powerful hair gels, waxes and fudges allowed for more crazy hairstyles, too. Women in the 60s had worn hair spray to keep their giant beehive hairdos in place. And special men's hairsprays were marketed to the mods and later the helmet-heads of the 70s. But the new products could keep your hair up in spikes like those of an allosaurus or stegosaurus, with a revival of interest in punk fashions from 20 years earlier. If parents and schools allowed them to, kids could colour their hair green or red or purple, or dust it with gold or silver. Most of these dyes washed out in a few days, but others kept their hair streaked permanently.

Later the skateboard look and tough grunge fashions from US prisons took hold. Men wore long shorts below the knee, very baggy tops, or trainers without laces and jeans so low that your undies showed. Hoodies came back from the 70s, but this time they had nothing to do with sports training: they were sloppy tops with hoods that were used to cover the face so no one could recognise you if you shoplifted or robbed a bank. They disturbed many adults because they seemed to symbolise withdrawal and isolation.

But it was also a time of glitz, too. Holidays became expensive 'escapes' instead of a week or two in a cottage at the beach. Shopping became 'retail therapy', pushed by the advertisers as good for boredom or depression. Most were just as bored or depressed after they'd shopped—especially when their credit card bill came in. But now going shopping was seen as a regular hobby, something girls or women would do together for fun.

Credit cards made this almost too easy. Cash—coins or notes—were used daily, and that was basically the only kind of money available to kids. Cheques were an ancient form of payment that were still in use, although there was always the danger that the person who wrote the cheque mightn't have enough money in their bank account to cover it, and the cheque would bounce. Now the easy availability of credit cards took away that worry.

Australia's first credit card—Bankcard—had been introduced in 1974. Many older Australians resisted it, because they had been brought up to save until you had the money to pay for something. Twenty years later the economy and attitudes had changed, the rules were relaxed (for better or worse) and some people had a wallet full of different credit cards. Once a bank issued you with a credit card you could buy things right up to your credit limit. Shop owners got their money and if you couldn't pay the credit card off at the end of the month, you paid interest on the loan to the bank who had issued you with the card.

It was great for shops. But many people became drunk on credit and ran up debts they could never pay. After all, there was so much new stuff to buy! Digital cameras that did all the hard work of focusing and judging light levels for you, so you only had to look and press. Video cameras, so you could make movies of your family; new computers in swish bright colours; cars with the new airbags for added safety if you crashed.

Four-wheel drives became popular at the same time. Many four-wheel drive fire trails were closed to stop overuse in national parks, but the big four-wheel drives were status symbols and most never drove off the bitumen, instead cruising round the cool inner-city suburbs. (They were supposed to be safer in crashes, but were in fact more likely to tip over.)

Australians wanted to keep their comfortable lives. And when John Howard became Australia's 25th prime minister on 11 March 1996, he promised to help them.

# CHAPTER 11

# TAXES, TIMOR AND TV

John Howard was a comfortable prime minister for a comfortable time. He promised to keep spending down, so that bank rates were lower, and taxes lower too, so that it was easier for families to pay the mortgages on their new bigger homes. He appealed to the Australians who were a bit nervous about the growing number of people who didn't come from an English-speaking background; who didn't care much if a TV show or a book was created in Australia or in the United States, and who felt vaguely sorry about the difficulties faced by Indigenous Australians, but didn't want to pay taxes to make their conditions better.

Just three weeks after John Howard was elected, the comfortable nation was horrified when a lone gunman shot down 35 people at the popular tourist site of Port Arthur in Tasmania. It wasn't a terrorist attack, but the act of a socially isolated and very disturbed young man, who was obsessed by guns. Howard moved swiftly. He got state and territory governments to pass uniform gun control legislation and put in place a federally funded gun buy-back scheme. Even his opponents were impressed.

## One Nation?

Pauline Hanson, a fish and chip shop owner, was elected Independent member for Ipswich, Queensland in 1996. She formed the One Nation Party in 1997, arguing that Australia shouldn't be multicultural and should stick to white, English migrants, as well as stop giving Indigenous people 'handouts'. She was saying what many believed, even if they hadn't said so publicly, but the effect was divisive. Her party gained more headlines than members, but by the end of the 90s it had vanished, mostly because of disagreements between party members and Pauline.

## JOHN WINSTON HOWARD

The son of a garage proprietor, John Winston Howard was born in Earlwood, Sydney in July 1939. He attended the local government primary school and later Canterbury Boys' High School, then graduated in law from Sydney University in 1961. He was elected to federal parliament as the Liberal party member for Bennelong in 1974, when Whitlam was prime minister.

Howard was Australia's second longest serving prime minister (Robert Menzies was in office for longer), serving for eleven years until the election of 24 November 2007. At that election he became only the second Australian prime minister to lose his own seat while in office. (The first was Stanley Bruce in 1929.) The hitherto safe Liberal seat seat was won by Labor candidate Maxine McKew.

Australia's economy grew and grew under John Howard. Paul Keating claimed that the growth was due to *his* economic reforms—he made them and John Howard got the credit. Howard said it was due to good management by the treasurer Peter Costello and himself, keeping government costs down. (In fact they kept creeping up, especially with Australia's involvement in the wars in Iraq and Afghanistan, and the growing social security costs as well as an enormous increase in middle-class welfare payments.)

Mostly it was because the world's major economies were booming—and while they boomed they wanted lots of Australia's minerals, such as coal, uranium, iron ore, gold, copper, silver and bauxite for aluminium.

Unemployment fell from over 8 per cent in 1996 to 5 per cent in 2005, inflation stayed pretty much under 3 per cent and interest rates were low enough for a couple on average wages to buy a house. (The days when one average income was enough to support a comfortable family had long gone.)

Many critics thought John Howard was trying to return Australia to the 1950s world of his hero, Menzies, and Howard did dismantle many of the laws of his predecessors. He changed labour laws so that unions no longer had the same power to strike if they felt conditions were unfair or wanted more money, and made it possible for many—or even most—workers to be employed on individual contracts, instead of on terms won for everyone on that job by the unions. Theoretically it meant that jobs could be much more flexible, but nearly always the new individual contracts made the job harder and involved working longer hours or for less money, and sometimes both.

Despite the fact that pastoralists did not lose any rights as a result of the Wik decision, many demanded that native title be extinguished on pastoral leases. In May 1997, the Howard government enacted a '10 Point Plan' that effectively wound back many of the rights recognised in the Native Title Act.

The Human Rights and Equal Opportunity Commission's Aboriginal and Torres Strait Islander Social Justice Commissioner, in his Native Title Report had this to say:

*The Wik decision provided our country with a potential basis for co-existence between Indigenous and non-Indigenous Australians. The Federal Government's Ten Point Plan destroyed that potential... Whichever way you look at these proposals it is impossible to find a just and fair framework which seeks to balance Australian property rights. You see bias. You see gross infringements of the human rights of Aboriginal and Torres Strait Islander peoples. You see 'bucket-loads of extinguishment'.*

The limits of the Native Title Act as it came to exist can be seen today in the small number of successful native title claims. Native title claims can take up to ten years to negotiate. Many of the successful claims are resolved through agreement between the government, land owners and traditional owners outside the framework of the Native Title Act and the courts. Addressing the limitations of this system and its overly legalistic nature remains a key part of the reconciliation movement today.

But although much criticised in the newspapers, these laws were fairly popular with most people. Their introduction was, after all, among the tasks Howard was elected to do. Then in the 1998 election he put forward an idea that most voters hated.

# The GST

Howard said he wasn't going to do it, and then he did. Paul Keating had wanted to introduce a consumption tax—paid whenever you bought something—but had been overruled by others in the Labor party. John Howard promised before he was elected in 1996 that he wouldn't introduce a GST (Goods and Services Tax). And he didn't—not that time.

But when he campaigned next time in 1998, John Howard offered Australia a new tax. Why on earth would anyone vote for someone who wanted to give them a new tax: 10 per cent on almost everything? They did, though, and Howard won the election.

The reason was partly that he promised to cut other taxes to compensate. It was also because many wealthy people used loopholes in the law to escape paying tax, either by being paid cash that the Australian Tax Office couldn't trace, or by forming legally complicated companies arranged so that they paid little or no tax at all. The GST would mean that everyone would have to pay *some* tax at least, whenever they bought anything.

But the victory was due to the fact that most Australians trusted John Howard. Few wanted the tax—but they preferred having John Howard and the tax, to the Labor Party and no tax.

Howard won again in 2001. The people who didn't like his policies felt things were getting worse and worse, especially as Howard seemed unconcerned about changes to the environment. Membership of groups including the Australian Conservation Foundation, Greenpeace, Friends of the Earth and the Greens political party all grew.

Perhaps Howard was right: most Australians weren't really interested. Most of the native title claims were a long way from the cities and didn't affect their lives. And most lives were more comfortable than ever before. Lifestyle shows, with ideas for renovating your home or garden, which fed society's obsession with 'nesting'—were the most popular programs on TV.

And then something else riveted Australians to their TV screens—violence in the small nation of East Timor, to our north.

## East Timor

Timor-Leste/East Timor had been a Portuguese colony and many Australians remembered the extraordinary bravery of the Timorese as they helped protect and hide Australian soldiers from the Japanese troops who occupied the country in World War II.

In 1975 Indonesia took over the country, against the wishes of many Timorese. The Australian government kept out of it, even when our journalists were killed by Indonesian troops as they tried to film what was happening.

But many Asian economies, including Indonesia, were in trouble in the 1997–98 Asian bubble collapse. In 1999 East Timor was going to have a referendum on whether it wanted to be independent or stay with Indonesia. The referendum was violent and bloody and after the answer was a resounding 'Yes' vote for independence, Indonesian troops and Indonesian trained and armed Timorese militias began slaughtering anyone who opposed them in scenes that horrified the world.

John Howard acted swiftly. Within days plans were put into place; within weeks troops were mobilised. Australia became one of the leaders of the United Nations International Force East Timor (INTERFET).

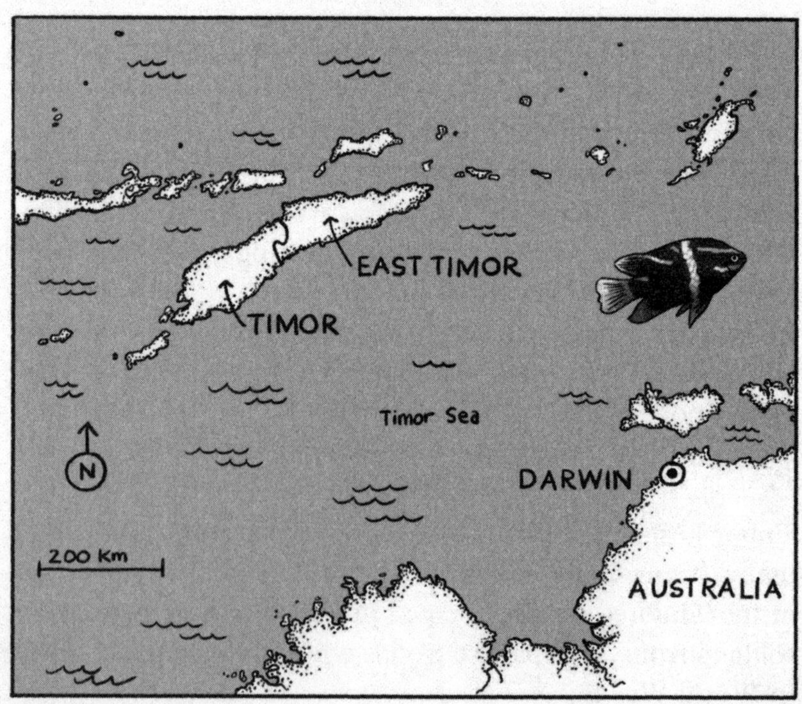

## Stabilisation

Australian personnel stayed in East Timor, assisting the government in various roles, including Operation SPIRE which saw two rotations of a Support Company of Engineers and Logisticians, until the final Australian withdrawal in May 2005.

In April and May 2006 more forces were sent to help the Government of East Timor (Timor-Leste) keep order after the attempted assassination of East Timor's prime minister (later president), Jose Ramos Horta, in February. Australia was part of the the United Nations International Stabilisation Force (ISF) which supported police operations by the UN Police (UNPOL) contingent, with officers from 20 other countries and Force Protection Units from Portugal, Malaysia, Pakistan and Bangladesh.

## Keeping the Peace

Australia had more or less forgotten its military heroes—except on Anzac Day—after the bitterness and differing opinions over the war in Vietnam, and the feeling of many Australians that the Gulf War had been fought to get access to oil, not to liberate Kuwait.

Yet the Gulf War had been just one of many, many places where Australians had recently served. Our forces were increasingly becoming 'peacekeepers', responding to emergencies across the world. Few Australians even knew that in the 1970s, 80s and 90s Australians had served courageously in many desperate war-torn areas, often as part of United Nations peacekeeping forces.

The following are just some of the areas where Australian forces were involved. An Australian force was part of Commonwealth Monitoring Force, Rhodesia (CMFR) 1979–1980, as Zimbabwe won its independence. Australians served with the Commonwealth Military Training Team in the civil war-torn Uganda (CMTTU) 1982–1984. From 1982 to 1986, and then from 1993 onwards, Australia was part of the Multinational Force and Observers in the Sinai. From 1989 to 1993 Australians too risked their lives as part of the dangerous—even life-threatening—work of the United Nations Mine Clearance Training Team in Pakistan and Afghanistan. From 1991 to 1994 Australian signallers helped with the United Nations Mission for the Referendum in Western Sahara.

By 1993, Australia had over 2,000 peacekeepers in the field, often working among scenes of horror, starvation and utter devastation, to give what help they could.

From 1993 to 1999 Australians worked with the United Nations Military Liaison Team/Cambodian Mine Action Centre, where civil war had left unexploded mines throughout the country—mines that could explode at any time, killing and maiming innocent people, even children playing in the fields. From 1992 to 1997 Australians were part of the United Nations peacekeeping activities in the former Yugoslavia, and in 1999, too, Australians served with the NATO force in Kosovo, trying to help protect the people of a country torn apart by civil war and genocide.

From 1992 to 1994 Australian troops went with the UN mission to drought- and war-ravaged Somalia. From 1994–1996 defence personnel served in the horror of Rwanda, where two major tribes tried to exterminate one another, killing millions and leaving millions more desperate and starving, and from 1994 to 2002 they worked with United Nations forces to try to make the land safe from unexploded land mines.

Australians were part of the NATO Stablisation Force in the former Republic of Yuguslavia, amid civil war and attempted genocide; part of the 1997 United Nations Survey Team in the Congo. From 1997–1998 our forces helped with drought assistance in Papua-New Guinea and the Irian Jaya (now West Papua) province of Indonesia. In 1998, too,

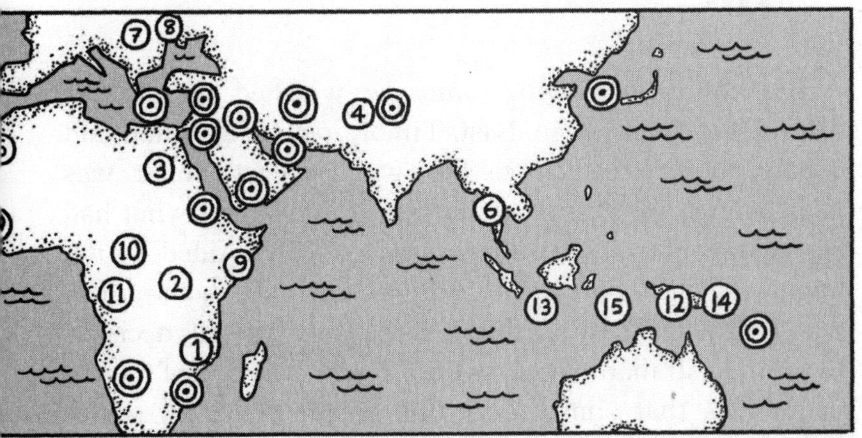

Australians helped after two or even three massive tsunamis hit the coast of Papua-New Guinea, killing and injuring many, and leaving others homeless.

From 1997 to 2003, Australians supported the Truce Monitoring Group/Peace Monitoring Group in Bougainville, that was trying to find peace in the long-running war between the New Guinea government and Bougainvilleans, who wanted their island to be an independent nation.

Few Australians knew that our forces took part in all these actions—or cared.

But now in our living rooms we watched our soldiers defend the helpless in East Timor, restoring order and overseeing free elections. The war in East Timor was near enough for journalists to film it and report what had been happening in newspapers and on TV. Aided by the popularity of the charismatic Major General Peter Cosgrove, who led the INTERFET mission, the government's decision to send Australian troops to East Timor was one of its few major acts that almost everyone supported. Even critics of John Howard felt he had acted decisively and made Australia proud that we were a nation who could and would act to help others.

The problems in East Timor were going to be harder to solve in the long term than most Australians realised. But at least we had done our best, and been there when we were needed. At the end of 1999, we were feeling pretty good.

It looked like the next millennium was going to be wonderful—unless the whole of civilisation ended on 1 January 2000.

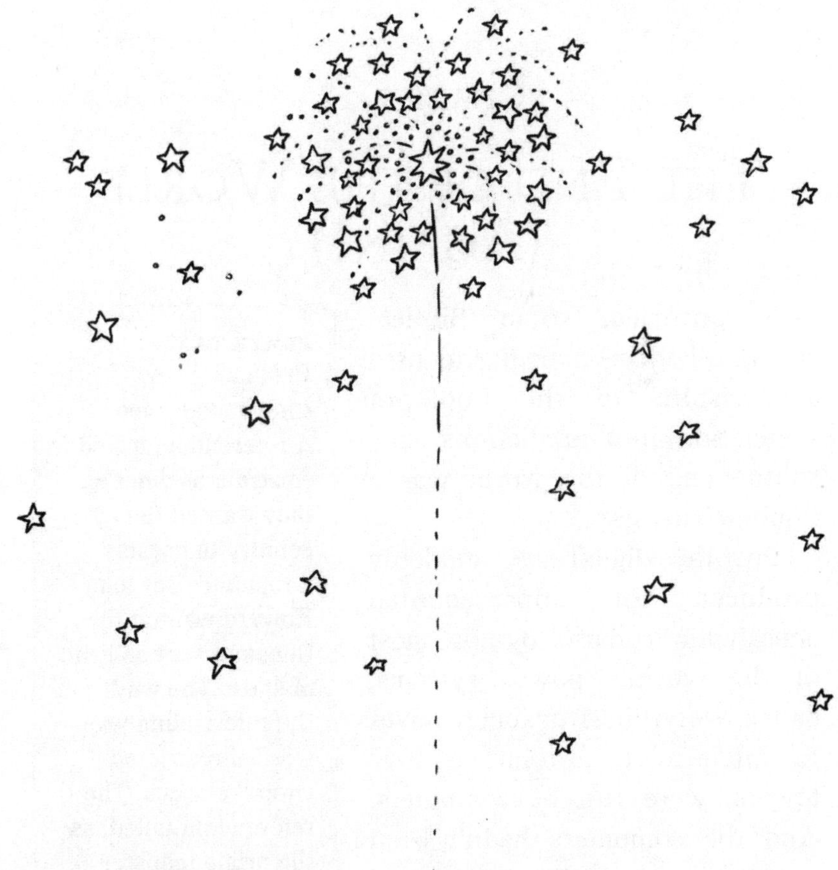

## CHAPTER 12

# THE END OF THE WORLD (AGAIN!)

For centuries, some Biblical scholars had been trying to turn the visions of the Book of Revelation into predictions, too, so the end of the world was a familiar business.

But the digital age suddenly produced an unprecedented apocalyptic scenario. By now most of the world's power systems, banks, everything from microwaves in kitchens to aircraft control towers, were run by computers. And the computers hadn't been programmed for a date that started with the numerals '20-'.

**POWER TO THE PEOPLE?**

**6 NOVEMBER 1999**

**A referendum asked Australians whether they wanted the country to become a republic. But John Howard wanted the Queen to stay as head of state. The way the referendum was worded restricted voters' choices. The referendum failed, as the prime minister had hoped it would.**

The Y2K bug, as the media called it, was a tiny glitch—but observers theorised that, because of it, bank accounts would vanish as computers crashed, planes tumble to the ground, cash registers fail to work in supermarkets…

Many people hoarded food and cash, at least to last them for a few weeks till things got back to normal. Some were petrified. But even more were preparing for one great enormous party. The clock clicked down to midnight on the last day of 1999. The fireworks boomed and crashed across the world, as one country after another entered the year 2000.

There were no crashing computers. The millennium bug had been firmly stomped on by computer programmers across the world, who fixed the systems before there could be any trouble. It seemed, nevertheless, that we were constantly on the lookout for an apocalypse.

The millennium bug wasn't wacky, like the aliens about to bring us peace and prosperity. It was real, a problem. But it was also a problem that people could solve—and they did. By dawn on 1 January the world knew it had survived into the next millennium.

**APOCALYPSE, LATER**

**Ten years later, in January 2010, some major computer systems did crash, because the programmers hadn't updated the systems well enough for them to cope with a '10'. But the problems were soon fixed.**

## CHAPTER 13

# THE NOUGHTIES

But what were they going to call the baby? No one was quite sure what to call this new decade, now that the 90s were over. Some people called them the 'noughties'; others simply talked about 'the new millennium'. And life was new—far different from the way humans had lived before. For those with access to the new digital devices and new communication platforms, at least, people were becoming citizens of the world, following international news, fashions and celebrities, willing to let new inventions change their way of life dramatically.

A few decades earlier, families had lived mostly in the kitchen, sitting around the table to prepare meals, eat, talk or play board and paper games. Later, families lived pretty much in their 'family room' eating or watching TV together, with little kids playing where their parents could keep an eye on them.

Now members of the family might spend a lot more time in their own room or the study, playing computer games or surfing the net, watching their own TV or DVD, listening to their iPod, where once the whole family had listened to the same piece of music together—or had sung it together, while one member played the piano or violin.

Kids had long since stopped playing in the street. In warm parts of Australia they might go over to a friend's house to swim in their pool; they'd text or email each other, or talk on their mobile phones.

And new social networking sites started to spring up all over the internet. Friendships were still close—but people had different ways of being with their friends.

Holidays were different, too.

A century earlier, only rich people had gone away on holidays or owned and rented holiday houses at the beach or the snow. Others were lucky to spend a day visiting the beach. In the 1920s and 30s working class and middle class Australians took up camping in tents or caravans—often homemade. By the 50s there were small fibro shacks up and down the coast that families rented for part of the school holidays, often without hot water and with a toilet out the back door.

By the 70s and 80s a lot more families had holiday homes, often rented out to tourists when they weren't using them, more comfortable ones with indoor toilets.

But Australians had grown even richer (again without realising in most cases just how much their standard of living had risen). Holidays were often taken now in luxury resorts with air-conditioning, heated swimming pools, spas and holiday clubs for the kids. It was often cheaper to fly to an exotic resort in Thailand or Bali, than to have a resort holiday in Australia.

Instead of making their own holiday fun, a large number of people bought it ready-made, just like the ready-made frozen pizzas they bought at the supermarket. There were theme parks in all the major cities and coastal holiday areas, where you could spend the whole day—and a lot of money—taking rides or seeing shows. If you wanted to go canoeing you'd go with a tour company, who organised the whole trip for you.

Once Australians had travelled overseas for adventure and to see the world, or for the jobs, fame and money they couldn't find back home. Now families jetted off for ten days of pampering.

Lifestyle shows made out that you could completely transform your house or garden in just two days. (They didn't mention the army of workers who were not on camera, and the endless hours of filming that it took to make it all look like a breeze.)

It was a richer, more affluent world. But it came at a price.

## A Cramped and Noisy World

Cities were polluted, noisy, and cramped, with traffic snarls and not much room to play. But the changes had come about so gradually that most Australians didn't realise things had grown so bad.

It was much more fun to party. Mathematicians pointed out that we were so keen, we were in fact a year early, and the new millennium didn't really begin till 2001. But no one cared. Even though the New Year celebrations were over, Australia still had a great big party to come.

## The 2000 Sydney Olympic Games

The first Olympic Games to be held in Australia had been in 1956 in Melbourne, in the days when competitors were still amateurs who'd trained in their spare time, and were billeted out to Melbourne people's homes. It had been the first TV games for Australians, and our competitors had won a swag of medals.

The Sydney games were supposed to be the biggest and best the world had seen! But would they be? For months, gossip said that the new roads, stadiums and other event stages would never be ready in time. The whole thing would be a disaster!

But it wasn't. Even the weather stayed perfect from the Opening Ceremony at 7 pm on Friday 15 September 2000, to the Closing Ceremony at 8 pm, Sunday, 1 October. It seemed everyone in Sydney was smiling. The trains were clean and ran on time, for once you could actually hear what was being announced over the public address system and guides helped you find the right gate when you got to the venue. Thousands of Australians volunteered to help direct the tourists around the city. The atmosphere was like an enormous party—the climax being when Indigenous sprinter, Cathy Freeman, won gold, pounding out ahead of the other competitors in her silver running suit, then dropping to the track and sitting there, taking it all in, while Australians wept and cheered.

And then the party was over, leaving a vast empty stadium and enormous debts that crippled New South Wales, with little funding to spare for schools, trains and hospitals.

## CHAPTER 14

# CHILDREN OVERBOARD!

John Howard was to win his third election in 2001. But despite the enormous continuing electoral support for Howard and his government, criticism was growing, too. There was even a feeling that he might have cheated a bit to try to win the election. It was all about kids—kids who had been thrown into the ocean by their parents. Or had they?

The children at the centre of the controversy were 'boat people'.

In 1989, boat people again started arriving, with the first group of arrivals coming from Cambodia. More would come from countries suffering war, civil disturbance and repression, including Iraq, Afghanistan, Iran and recently Sri Lanka and Myanmar/Burma. In most cases these asylum seekers had paid huge sums of money to people smugglers, who crammed people into often unseaworthy boats.

Once again a lot of media space was given to the refugees coming by boat—ignoring the fact that far more asylum seekers and illegal immigrants came by plane, on tourist visas. John Howard called the boat people 'queue jumpers' trying to take the places of people who had gone through the right channels. But for many of the people trying to come here, there were no embassies, or safety, to give them the chance to apply. Some were the wives or children of asylum seekers already in Australia—one reason why the small, often leaky or collapsing boats held so many women and small children.

The asylum seeker issue became front page news in the months before the 2001 election. In August 2001, a Norwegian freighter, the *MV Tampa*, rescued 433 refugees from a sinking boat outside Australia's territorial waters and started to head towards the detention and processing centre on Christmas Island. The Australian government refused the *Tampa* permission to enter Australia waters. On 29 August, concerned about the health of the asylum seekers, the captain of the *Tampa* proceeded towards Christmas Island anyway. As soon as the ship entered Australian territorial waters, it was boarded by Australian defence forces.

John Howard was adamant—the *Tampa* asylum seekers would not be allowed onto Australian soil. But what was

going to happen to them? There wasn't room on the ship—or enough food, water and medical assistance. And, anyway, it was hardly Norway's responsibility: the captain had only been trying to help in an emergency.

Headlines flashed around the world, criticising the Australian government. Norway and international agencies, too, demanded that Australia allow people rescued at sea to land on its shores.

Meanwhile, the asylum seekers were still on board the ship. The Australian government quickly passed legislation and brokered a deal with the Pacific island of Nauru. It cost Australian taxpayers $1 billion to get rid of the problem. Nauru needed the money, since it had stopped the mining of bird droppings for fertilisers that had been its main source of income. This deal became known as the Pacific Solution. Nauru—and later Papua-New Guinea, particularly Manus Island—became the bases for offshore facilities to 'process' asylum seekers. The government also introduced a policy—Operation Relex—which charged Australian navy vessels with the duty of intercepting boats loaded with asylum seekers and turning them back to Indonesia.

The asylum seekers were taken off the *Tampa* and transported to Nauru, or in some cases New Zealand, to await assessment of their refugee status.

As the election grew closer, the Howard government declared that it had shown it was strong on border protection. Now there seemed to be an even greater need to control immigration. 'We will decide who comes to this country,' Howard declared, 'and the circumstances in which they come.'

For half a century the bad guys were supposed to be the Communists: the Communists of Russia, or the countries they controlled as part of the USSR, the Communist Chinese, Vietnamese Communists. But now there appeared to be another enemy—and most frightening, they weren't a country; just those who followed a particular fanatical belief.

## The War on Terror

On the morning of 11 September 2001, in a well-orchestrated exercise, Al-Qaeda suicide pilots flew two hijacked commercial planes into the twin towers of the World Trade Centre in lower Manhattan and changed the course of world politics. A third plane was flown into the Pentagon, the US Defence Department headquarters in Washington DC, and a fourth crashed before reaching the White House, its likely target. About 3,000 people died. Al-Qaeda, a radical Islamist organisation headed by Saudi Arabian, Osama bin Laden, vowed to wipe out US colonialism, bases and business across the world, and turn the planet into a fundamentalist Islamic state.

John Howard was in Washington at the time of the attacks, and with tears in his eyes grieved along with the American people for those they had lost. Many Australians, too, felt not just sympathy, but the sorrow you would feel if a member of your family or a neighbour had been hurt.

But it wasn't just grief. The attacks seemed to have come from nowhere. Would there be more? Al-Qaeda had promised there would be. But what? And when? And how could you fight an enemy that could be anywhere and nowhere?

A package found in the US mail containing powdered anthrax made the West nervous about letter-borne threats, too. Parcels were scanned; packages of suspicious white powder opened by men in protective bio-hazard suits—and found to be something harmless like washing powder.

US President George W Bush declared a 'war on terrorism' and John Howard pledged his support. New security measures led to long security queues at airports; disposable razors and even nail files were banned. Cosmetics and after-shave had to be in small sizes only and sealed in a plastic bag separated from your luggage for scanning. Soon you would no longer be able to take any liquid on an international flight, in case it was a liquid explosive.

John Howard aligned himself closely with George W Bush, who called him Australia's 'man of steel'. Australia sent troops to support the US-led invasion of Afghanistan, where the militant Islamist Taliban controlled much of the country, funded by the enormously wealthy illegal drugs trade, where Al-Qaeda leaders could be training supporters and bin Laden was reportedly hiding. As I write this book in 2010, Australians are still serving in Afghanistan.

Al-Qaeda declared that Australia, too, was the enemy.

Then on 6 October 2001, a small wooden boat carrying 223 asylum seekers on *SIEV 4* (Suspected Illegal Entry Vessel 4) was found by an Australian navy vessel north of Christmas Island. By now many Australians were suspicious of any foreigners trying to get into the country illegally. But were they really illegal? If they were genuine refugees, under United Nations treaties to which Australia was a signatory, they had a right to find safety.

Australian government ministers claimed that asylum seekers had set the boat alight and thrown their children overboard to try to have them rescued by an Australian ship and so be granted asylum in Australia. Blurry photos that appeared to prove this were given to the Australian media just days before the election.

What sort of people would throw their own kids into the ocean? How could we possibly have people like that coming here? Old racist prejudices began to grow stronger once again. What if these people were terrorists in disguise? Hostility towards the asylum seekers grew, as well as support for the government in its efforts at border control.

It had looked like John Howard might lose the 2001 election. But the 'children overboard' story and his swift action changed public opinion so much that his government was returned at the election on 10 November 2001 with an increased majority.

But had the kids really been thrown overboard? There had been claims before the election that the pictures were of another ship that was sinking and the parents and kids had been forced into the sea. There were other claims that the parents were so frightened of warning shots fired above their ship that they had jumped into the sea with their kids to save them. These asylum seekers had come from violent war-torn countries, and had no way of knowing that the shots were being fired above their ship, not at them with the intention of killing them.

What had really happened?

A Senate Select Committee Inquiry later found that no children were thrown overboard and that the government had known this prior to the election. John Howard's reputation for honesty had taken a hit, but too late for the 2001 election. The *SIEV 4* had been towed towards Christmas Island, but when it began to sink a couple of days later, the asylum seekers were rescued and taken on board *HMAS Adelaide*.

And now another asylum seeker tragedy was revealed. The tiny 19-metre *SIEV X* had left Sumatra in Indonesia with about 400 people on board. It was incredibly overcrowded and leaking badly. A day later, on 19 October 2001, it sank in international waters in the Indian Ocean and 353 people drowned. Many of the survivors had been in the water for more than 20 hours.

Did the navy know the boat was coming to Australia? Was there a ship close enough to have rescued the passengers? Or was nothing done, simply to make sure that no more 'queue jumpers' arrived before the election?

There are no clear answers. The case of the *SIEV X*—just like the knowledge that the 'boat people' had never thrown their kids over the side—didn't come out until after the election. Nor was there any way of verifying whether John Howard had known that the 'children overboard' story was true or not.

In 2004 there was another election and, once more, John Howard won comfortably. At this election, the government parties gained a majority in the Senate for the first time since 1981. Now Howard was free to change Australia without having to convince Green or Independent senators to help pass his new laws.

## A New Australia Online

Australia was increasingly a small part in a bigger world picture. Our entertainment mostly came from overseas. Much of our information did, too. Australians still bought newspapers and watched the news on TV. But in 2001, Jimmy Wales founded Wikipedia, a community-run internet encyclopedia. He had a vision of a world in which every single person on the planet had free access to the sum of all human knowledge. Everyone would be free to add information to Wiki, as it became known, or to correct information. It was free, and had no advertising.

Not all of its information was accurate or reliable. But as the decade progressed, more and more Australians would use search engines like Google to find the information they wanted on the internet instead of looking it up in books.

Shopping sites like eBay meant that you could both buy and sell items without leaving home—or even on your laptop while you were on the bus or the train.

Families changed, too. Most mums worked outside the home, either full-time or part-time and a high proportion of them headed single-parent families. Dads helped in the house—though it was mostly the women still organising who did what and doing all the bits left over. Young men could cook as well as young women did—which sometimes wasn't very much. Why peel, boil and mash potatoes when you could buy a frozen pizza? Most city houses had a list of places that delivered take-away meals, or where you could at least drive and pick up food to bring home.

Australians had become health conscious, because they were aware of the dangers in their sedentary occupations, sitting in front of a screen most of the day. But they grew tired of being lectured about it. So many of them ate healthy food for part of the week and take-aways or junk food for the rest.

The most common Australian breakfast was packaged cereal—quick to buy, serve and eat—with lots of sugar in it. Adults took coffee seriously, visiting their favourite coffee bar for a take-away espresso or cappuccino in a paper cup. TVs were getting bigger, and now you could have 'pay' TV, too, as well as the free-to-air, with many channels of sport, movies and cartoons. You could buy cheap DVDs to watch, or you could rent them for a dollar a night.

It was still a comforting, comfortable time for most.

And then it changed once again.

# The War on Terror in our Backyard

On 12 October 2002, 202 people, 88 of them Australians, were killed when a bomb went off in a popular tourist bar in Bali; ten seconds later a car outside exploded, killing those who were trying to flee, as yet another bomb went off outside the US Embassy, though this injured only one person.

There were extraordinary acts of heroism as Balinese and Australians risked their lives to help the wounded. But it brought home to all Australians the realisation that Australia's position in world politics would have repercussions for us all.

Australia was no longer safely far away at the bottom of the world.

In February 2003, the Foreign Minister Alexander Downer released a white paper providing a framework for Australia's foreign policy. This highlighted the importance the government placed on Australia's relations with the United States and the significance of terrorism and security and security issues in forging foreign policy. The paper referred to the government's concern over 'the growth of Islamic extremism and terrorism in South-East Asia'. And it said that there was no choice but to fight terrorism, with Iraq and North Korea specially seen as threats to world peace.

President Bush claimed that Saddam Hussein had weapons of mass destruction that could attack the world's major cities in hours, with nuclear warheads and biological weapons. The United States along with Australia and other allies were still fighting in Afghanistan. But now Bush said it was vital that Saddam Hussein be stopped before he could attack the West.

## THE SECOND GULF WAR

A month later the Australian government agreed to a request by President Bush to send Australian forces to Iraq as part of a 'Coalition of the willing'. Bush hoped the invasion would be quick and successful. As a storm of cruise missiles and bombs rained down over several days, the war became a TV event with Westerners in their living rooms watching the missiles hit Baghdad.

Baghdad itself soon fell and President Bush stood in combat gear on the deck of the *USS Abraham Lincoln* before a banner titled 'Mission Accomplished' and claimed victory—prematurely, as it turned out. Bringing peace to the country was going to prove hard.

As this book is being written in 2010, United States troops are withdrawing from Iraq. Australia withdrew most of its forces in August 2009, although there are still troops in Iraq conducting security duty for the Australian Embassy in Baghdad.

Almost 14,000 Australian troops served in Iraq and three Australians died. Saddam Hussein was executed for crimes against humanity, condemned by the mass graves of those he had put to death, and the minority groups he tried to annihilate. In 2009 more than 90 per cent of Iraqi voters turned out for democratic elections. But Iraq is still a long way from peace.

Many critics declared there was no evidence for the claims that there were weapons of mass destruction and that the war was more about securing access to oil for the US (and Australia) and keeping Saudi Arabia stable, than freeing Iraqis from the reign of the dictator Saddam Hussein.

The weapons of mass destruction mightn't have existed, but the threat from terrorism did. John Howard increased funding for intelligence agencies, aviation, maritime and border security and regional counter-terrorism measures and introduced about 28 new federal anti-terrorism laws, including the ASIO Amendment Act 2003, which allowed for seven-day detention without charge of suspects. Some people felt the new laws were going to be an even greater threat to Australians' freedom than terrorism. But most people once again felt the laws would have little or no effect on their lives.

During the next few years in the civilian arena, Howard's belief in mutual obligation between recipients of support and the government also led to far-reaching changes in social welfare, including:

- a 'work for the dole' scheme that linked unemployment relief to recipients' willingness to work at assigned tasks
- the abolition of the Aboriginal and Torres Strait Islander Commission (ATSIC) in June 2004 and transfer of ATSIC programs to mainstream agencies, with shared responsibility agreements introduced in 2005 in which Indigenous communities defined the changes they would implement in return for government funding.

Australia's role in the Pacific was maintained, with significant military and police assistance to East Timor and Tonga, and continued assistance to Papua-New Guinea. In July 2003, with growing violence in the Solomon Islands, Australia led the Regional Assistance Mission to Solomon Islands (RAMSI) to help keep order. As with East Timor, there were no quick solutions, but there was still an overwhelming feeling that life would be a lot worse for the people of those countries if Australia wasn't there, helping.

In 2005 the Australian defence forces helped in Sumatra after a devastating tsunami, and in Pakistan after a massive earthquake, as well as a project in 2007 in the tiny Island nation of Kiribati to get rid of unexploded devices left there in World War II.

Now that John Howard was able to get laws through both the House of Representatives and the Senate, he could make even more radical changes, moving to get rid of compulsory trade union membership and restructuring industrial relations, including the replacing of award wages with direct employer-employee enterprise bargaining; replacing the Commonwealth Employment Service with a privatised system of employment service providers; and privatising the national telecommunications company, Telstra, by selling 49 per cent of the company—despite protests from people in rural Australia that they would be even less likely to get the phone service they desperately needed from a private company. Slowly but steadily the services Australians had taken for granted, like a public phone box on the corner, disappeared.

## The Stolen Generations

But there was one thing John Howard wouldn't do, and that was to apologise to Indigenous Australians for the treatment they had suffered in the past and the suffering that continued.

In 1987 a Royal Commission into Aboriginal Deaths in Custody had been set up to try to stop deaths by suicide and the bashing of so many Indigenous people in jail. Its 1991 report painted a terrible picture of the unequal position of Indigenous people in Australia.

Partly in response to the findings of that Royal Commission, the federal parliament established the Council for Aboriginal Reconciliation in 1991, which had as its goal the 'transformation of Aboriginal and non-Aboriginal relations in this country'. Reconciliation groups were set up around the country and the Council put out a final report in 2000. Among other recommendations, it proposed that the government initiate a process to unite Australians through a formal agreement or treaty.

But the Howard government rejected any moves towards a treaty.

In 1995 the Human Rights and Equal Opportunity Commission began a National Inquiry into the Separation of Aboriginal and Torres Strait Islander Children from their Families. The report, *Bringing them Home*, was released in 1997. It painted a devastating picture of the ongoing impact of a government policy from around 1910 to the 1960s that removed Indigenous children from their families and placed them in institutions.

Sometimes—even often—this was done to save the children from starvation or injury; at other times and in other places it was done from a feeling that children with any white ancestry were best brought up away from their Indigenous families, or even a feeling that it would be best if the 'inferior' black races died out. The children involved came to be known as the Stolen Generation, although far more than one generation was affected. Many of those children experienced abuse and cruelty in the institutions that were supposed to care for, educate and nurture them. (Abuse and cruelty happened in orphanages and schools for 'white' kids too: at last the world was beginning to listen to the stories of the survivors.)

The 'stolen generations' was a complex story, with many, many motives for taking children away from their communities. But it had hastened the destruction of Indigenous culture, as children were brought up away from their families and their land.

Mr Howard consistently refused to apologise to the stolen generations. He rejected what he called the 'black armband view of history' and stressed instead Australia's 'remarkably positive history'.

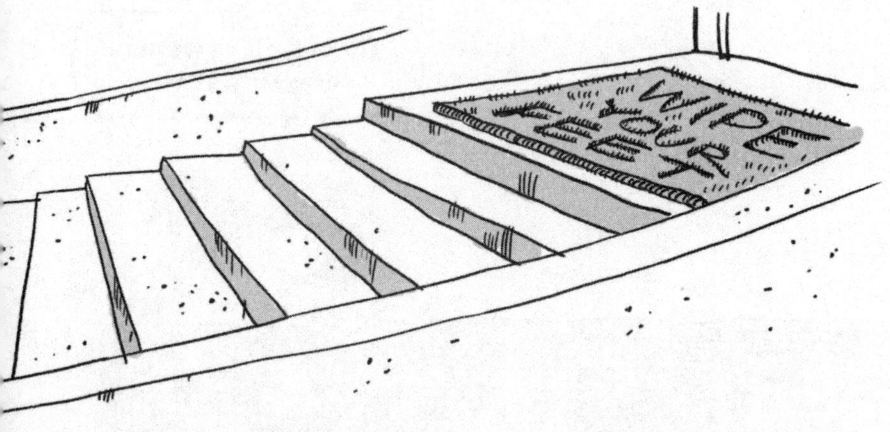

On 26 May 2000, more than 250,000 people walked across Sydney Harbour Bridge in support of Indigenous Australians prior to Corroboree 2000, which was held at the Opera House the following day to endorse the Reconciliation Council's Australian Declaration Towards Reconciliation. The Sydney Harbour Bridge walk was followed by walks in other capital cities around Australia.

## Australia Warms and Burns

John Howard continued to say no to something else, too—the possibility that the world was getting hotter. Far-off glaciers and ice caps were melting; *El Nino* was part of the language and Australian droughts were becoming longer and more frequent.

But he refused to sign the Kyoto Protocol—an agreement worked out between nations at Kyoto to try to reduce greenhouse gas emissions and help stop the world getting hotter.

Climate change didn't just mean a warmer world. It meant that the great ocean currents would change direction and speed. Some places might freeze. Ice caps would melt so the oceans would rise, flooding river deltas where many of the world's great cities had grown, and low-lying farmland.

The land of Australia and its people had faced extraordinary challenges before: the massive floods at the end of the last Ice Age, which had created Bass Strait and separated Tasmania and most of our islands from the continent. Now it looked like we, or our children, might face similar dramatic climate changes.

Large parts of many cities, built around rivers and lakes and along the coast, were only just above water level; many were below it, and so far protected by sand dunes. But if big storms ripped away the sand dunes, many kilometres might be flooded in a few days—just as the land had been 10,000 years before.

1995 had seen another drought in south-eastern Australia. The 2002–2004 drought was worse. Not just because it rained less. Most parts of Australia had been getting a reduced rainfall over the past 20 years, even when it hadn't been a declared drought. Dams had emptied. The water table was lower.

There were a lot more of us, too—and we were using more water per head. Our homes were bigger. We had swimming pools and spas, and used lots of appliances so we needed lots of power—and the power stations used lots of water to generate it. So did mining and manufacturing. Giant cotton farms like Cubbie Station used massive amounts of water to grow cotton, one of the most water-hungry crops on Earth in one of the driest lands.

For the first time Australians in cities had to face the fact that there just wasn't enough water for everyone—not if we were going to keep using it as lavishly as we had been. Local councils imposed regulations to stop people using so much water. Sprinklers were banned. When times were bad gardens could only be watered a day or two a week, and then strictly by hand.

But most of the water people used didn't come directly from their taps. It was used to grow their food, to produce their power or the clothes they wore. Australians began to face the task of managing one of the most essential resources for survival.

Drought and high temperatures brought other terrors, too—hot, gale-force winds—and bushfire.

## Canberra Burns

On 18 January 2003, when many Canberra families were holidaying at the coast, 'bushfire' suddenly became 'city fire' as at least 160 separate fires that had been burning for nearly two weeks after lightning strikes in the Kosciuszko, Namadgi and Brindabella national parks west of the city approached Canberra. Strong winds pushed them faster, and faster still. Although to some residents and many New

South Wales bushfire crews it seemed inevitable that the fires would reach Canberra that day, the Australian Capital Territory emergency services told people who rang up not to panic, and not to believe the scaremongers; it was all fine.

It wasn't.

By lunchtime the emergency headquarters had been burned. With no one directing the emergency response—and waiting New South Wales fire crews not being given permission to come into the ACT—ABC presenter Julie Derret and her producer and the ABC receptionist took mobile calls from people in the burning suburbs, marked out the burning areas on a map on the floor, reassured people and gave the most accurate information possible about what was happening.

The sky grew dark. Even 100 km away it was as though night had fallen—a night that even torches couldn't light, a night of ash. Many separate fires burned that day and for weeks afterwards, some lit as control fires before Christmas, then left to burn and kill.

Australia had faced horrific fires before. But not fire with this heat and these winds. Four people died, a total of 470 homes were destroyed and 2,000 businesses, homes and vehicles were damaged.

The death toll was less than many other bushfires. But this was a capital city, not a country town or houses in the bush. The failure of official emergency services to warn or act was as frightening as the fire itself.

The 2003 drought and bushfires made many Australians realise exactly what global warming meant to us.

And there was another area in which doing nothing had major consequences. The development was so slow and gradual that few realised it was happening till it was too late.

Australia's population was growing: but the infrastructure—the network of road and rail systems, the schools, the hospitals—wasn't growing fast enough to cope. In fact, allowing for rising costs, infrastructure was getting less and less money. Mostly the problem was invisible: people slowly grew used longer waiting times for surgery, crowding in schools and shabby trains. But by 2007 a general feeling had developed that it was time for a fresh vision.

John Howard's coalition government lost office in the November 2007 election and the Labor party won with a 16-seat majority.

# CHAPTER 15

# KEVIN 07

## RUDD SAYS HE'LL SHOULDER THE BURDEN

All prime ministers since World War II had come from either New South Wales or Victoria. Kevin Michael Rudd broke the pattern. He was a Queenslander. From a poor family, who valued intelligence and good education, Kevin Rudd was born in the Queensland country town of Nambour in 1957, the son of a share farmer and a nurse. He went to Eumundi Primary School, then Marist College, Ashgrove and Nambour State High School and graduated from the Australian National University in Asian Studies in 1981. He joined the Labor Party at the age of 15 and was a career diplomat, speaking fluent Mandarin before being elected to federal parliament for the seat of Griffith in 1998.

Mr Rudd became leader of the ALP after challenging the then leader Kim Beazley in December 2006. He had been a friendly regular on breakfast television; unlike John Howard he was comfortable with networking sites on the internet, and young supporters campaigned in T-shirts with the American-style slogan 'Kevin 07' on them. Less than a year later he was prime minister.

But once again the ALP didn't control the Senate—and once again the Senate would refuse to pass the laws that the Labor prime minister wanted and for which his party felt it had an electoral mandate.

Rudd's first official act as prime minister was to ratify the Kyoto Protocol—immediately after being sworn in at Government House. His next act cost no money, but would be remembered as one of the most emotional days in many people's lives.

On 13 February 2008, just over two months after his election, Rudd captured the emotions and support of the nation with his apology to the stolen generations in Parliament House, Canberra. There were emotional scenes as crowds watched the apology on screens outside the building. The speech began:

*...today we honour the Indigenous peoples of this land, the oldest continuing cultures in human history.*

*We reflect on their past mistreatment.*

*We reflect in particular on the mistreatment of those who were stolen generations—this blemished chapter in our nation's history.*

*The time has now come for the nation to turn a new page in Australia's history by righting the wrongs of the past and so moving forward with confidence to the future.*

*We apologise for the laws and policies of successive parliaments and governments that have inflicted profound grief, suffering and loss on these, our fellow Australians.*

*We apologise especially for the removal of Aboriginal and Torres Strait Islander children from their families, their communities and their country…*

TV viewers around the country and around the world were inspired; the only disappointment for many was that the new government did not offer the stolen generations any financial compensation.

Still, a start had been made on the bold program of change that Labor had put to the people before the election. Rudd had promised an end to what were seen as the unfair industrial 'WorkChoices' laws brought in by John Howard. He pledged more money for schools and hospitals, a fairer and more caring Australia.

## The World Goes Bust!

But before much of this could happen the Western world's economy crashed. Many shares lost more than half their value—which meant that people's savings and superannuation were now worth only half of what they had been before—or even less. Banks across the world, but especially in the United States, Europe and Iceland, failed. It turned out that local councils in Australia had invested in some of these banks, as their interest rates were higher than those offered by Australian banks. Economists called it the Global Financial Crisis, but even at the local level, Australians were hit hard.

What had gone wrong? How could this have happened in just a few weeks?

The crisis started when two big government-backed mortgage companies in the United States failed. They had been lending money to people who couldn't pay it back, because they didn't have sufficient income to service the loan. The mortgage providers had relied that the price of housing would keep rising, so that if (or when) the borrower defaulted, the house could be sold to cover the amount of the loan. But the price of houses in the US began to fall.

That wasn't, however, the main cause. Over the past two decades, stock markets and the value put on businesses and land and houses had been rising steadily. Many people had borrowed too much to pay for stocks, houses or land, and had maxed out their credit cards to pay for holidays and big screen TVs. Basically the developed economies across the world had lots of people who had borrowed far more than they could ever pay back, and they had often borrowed to buy things like cars and TV sets that were not going to increase in value.

As the disaster unfolded in the US, people there lost their houses and jobs and ended up homeless on the streets. Rudd acted fast to stop Australia going under. He guaranteed that all deposits in Australian banks were safe to prevent people withdrawing all their funds from the banks—which would then make the banks fail. He put a temporary limit on the amounts people could withdraw from various other investments. He brought in a 'stimulus package' of government spending that gave most Australians cash to spend and also grants to schools and community groups for buildings and computers, and there was tax relief for businesses that bought anything new, from computers to cars.

It worked. By mid-2009 it looked like Australia was one of the few developed countries that avoided going into a major recession.

On 1 January 2010, Australia had new national employment standards and awards, including changing the 38-hour working week to include casuals, unpaid parental leave entitlements extended by up to 24 months, requests for flexible working arrangements and the right of certain employees to take redundancy.

Employers could no longer make individual workplace agreements with their staff. Australia's almost 4,000 state and federal awards were reduced to just under 130, to ensure minimum wages and working conditions for all Australian employees.

But Rudd's 'stimulus package' had cost a lot, and many election promises had been put on hold because of the crisis. Australia was in debt—and in 2010 stock markets across the world plunged again and then again with growing problems in Greece, Italy and the United States. There were complaints and scandals about how some of the 'stimulus package' money had been spent, too, with poor workmanship, deadly home insulation that electrocuted people, and school buildings that seemed wildly over-priced. It had been up to the states to inspect the insulation installations and manage the money for schools, but the federal government was still often blamed for the problems.

Many Australians still had no clear idea what areas the state, federal and local governments were responsible for. Like so many other prime ministers, Rudd was suddenly no longer as wildly popular as he had been.

It seemed like the world was full of problems—and so many solutions caused new problems to appear. Media reports were full of stories, not just about economic woes, but also earthquakes, volcanic eruptions, shrinking glaciers, vast clouds of air or sea pollution, and vanishing rivers.

## Black Saturday

By 2009 the long drought was beginning to feel like normal weather. Would the wet years ever return? January that year was hot; February was worse, and Victoria in particular was extraordinarily dry. Much of its forest was particularly flammable, the sort of forest that had grown back after many previous fires.

By early February there were bushfires around Australia. Most were brought under control, with little damage. But not in Victoria. 173 people died; 2,029 homes were burnt; whole towns turned to ash and smoke.

Australia watched their TV screens in shock and horror, then with overwhelming generosity gave money and goods to help the survivors. But once again the same questions were asked.

How had this tragedy happened? Why were there so few warnings—and in many cases, none? Why did the actual work of fighting fires still depend mostly on volunteers?

Once again, emergency services had failed to respond properly to the danger.

But mostly it was simply the extreme weather—unprecedented high temperatures and sudden extraordinarily strong winds that kept changing direction, so that it was hard to predict exactly where the fire might go next. Yet as in the Canberra fires, some houses in the areas of greatest destruction survived—partly because of the way they had been designed and built, or the clearing of firebreaks around them; partly because of the organised way the residents defended them.

Or was it luck?

Certainly both lots of fires showed that the policy of 'controlled burning'—the lighting of fires in winter and spring to reduce the amount of material that would burn—wasn't enough to stop major bushfires. In some places it could even make bushfires worse by encouraging plants that thrived in a fiery environment. In other places it might help a bit—but not enough when things were really bad. Bushfires were now a common part of life in this country—and the fires were going to get worse. After 200 years, non-Indigenous Australians were still learning how to live here. So it was time to think seriously, not just about surviving a bushfire, but about how we were going to live in a land of drought and flames.

The summer of 2010 brought another *El Niño* year, with drought spreading over eastern and southern Australia, although the newly understood Indian Ocean weather patterns were supposed to bring good rain to Western Australia. Nonetheless, fires ringed Perth and raced across the wheat belt over the 2009–2010 Christmas period, while floods devastated Queensland and northern and inland New South Wales; by January 2010 much of Australia was readying itself for bushfire again. February brought more floods.

Our land had changed, all right. The cities were crowded and clouded by pollution. Dust storms swept across the land, leaving homes and gardens red or grey. Fresh water was becoming increasingly scarce. Much of our living depended on food, clothes and gadgets that were imported from far away. And Australians jetted off for holidays in the Pacific as easily as their grandparents had driven 'down the coast'.

The world was growing hotter still, with no agreement at the 2009 Copenhagen talks on ways to turn back the fog of CO2. Kevin Rudd's promise to help secure an international accord on climate change had failed for the time being. He had even decided that there would be no Australian 'climate change' package within the next couple of years. Members of the opposition who had supported John Howard's inaction on this crucial challenge declared that they had been right after all in identifying themselves as 'climate change sceptics'.

# Chapter 16

# PMs Change; The Climate Changes More

By the time of the 21 August 2010 election, Australian politics was very different from the way it was a few months before. Despite Kevin Rudd's success in keeping Australia free from the desperate economic troubles in the United States and Europe, he had become increasingly unpopular, partly because he abandoned his climate change policy, partly because of insulation and building scandals under his 'stimulus plan', and partly because ALP officials felt he didn't consult others enough. In what seemed like an overnight decision that startled the public, the Labor Party replaced him as prime minister with Julia Gillard, making her Australia's first female prime minister. Within weeks, she called an election.

Julia Gillard was feisty and popular, but many voters felt uneasy about the way she had become prime minister.

Most women rejoiced that at last we had a woman in the job—but not enough to vote for her.

Julia Gillard and the Labor Party won 72 seats. Tony Abbott and the Liberal-National Party Coalition won 72 seats too, although a 'National Party Independent' in Western Australia also won a seat, so the Coalition claimed it had won 73. Four independent candidates and a member of the Greens Party won seats. The Greens would also hold the balance of power in the new Senate.

More than 5 per cent of Australians had not made proper marks on the ballot paper, so they were counted as 'informal'. Some of these may have been mistakes, but others were protest votes against the disappointing campaigns by both major parties. In a move that appeared to sum up the mood of the electorate, the major pre-election debate between the prime minister, Julia Gillard, and the leader of the opposition, Tony Abbott, had been rescheduled so it didn't clash with the final episode of Australia's most popular TV program, 'MasterChef'.

Even the prime minister acknowledged that Australians were less interested in the political future of their country than in cooking. And an unprecedented number of voters failed to vote at all—even though it is illegal not to vote in Australian elections.

While many voters approved of Tony Abbott, an unusual number declared they were voting Labor simply to keep him out of power. Other traditional Labor voters felt that Kevin Rudd had been betrayed. Of all Australian elections, this one seemed to leave voters the most frustrated, with a result that pleased no one—except the independents, the Greens and those who voted for them.

Neither the Labor Party nor the Liberal-National Coalition had convinced the Australian people to vote them into government with a majority. The closeness of the result showed how divided the country was on many important

issues. Seemingly endless negotiations followed the election, during which the major parties tried to persuade the independent and Greens members to support them, so they could form what is known as a 'minority government'.

The independents pointed out that the whole political scene had changed. Australians were sick of campaigns scripted by spin doctors. They wanted to hear a broader range of opinions, from politicians who said what they really believed, rather than what the marketing department had told them to say. Parliament would no longer be an arena in which the two major parties slugged it out. Question Time in parliament was for real questions and real answers—not the reading out of prepared media releases. Most of the independents also came from regional electorates. They said that for too long the city-based politicians had neglected the Bush. That had to change, too.

Even journalists who had been observing Australian politics for many years began to speak of a new era. Australians had voted for a more complex debate on such matters as climate change, immigration and taxes. As the independents said, it was time for co-operation. The leader of the opposition promised a kinder, gentler approach to differences of opinion.

After more than two weeks of negotiations, three of the independent members and the Greens member announced that they would enable Julia Gillard to form a government. This would give the Labor Party a potential 76 votes out of the 150 votes in the House of Representatives: a majority of one. The independents emphasised that they were not endorsing all Labor's policies, and they reserved the right to vote against them. They wanted a fairer deal for regional Australia and to see stable government get going again.

THE THREE COUNTRIES OF AUSTRALIA

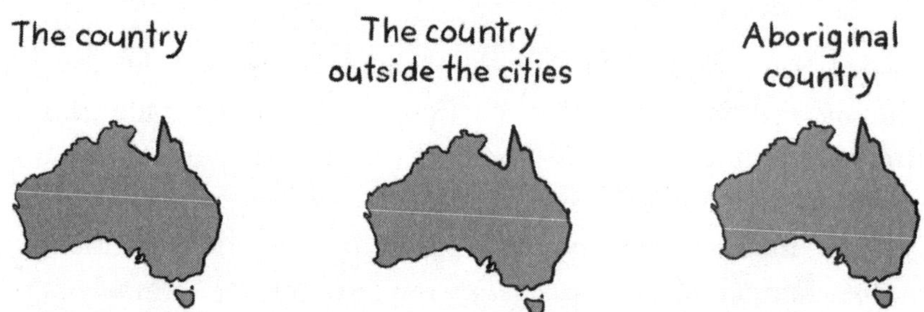


So on 7 September 2010, Julia Gillard was confirmed as Australia's prime minister. The following day, journalists were talking about the 'two sides' of politics once again. One Coalition shadow minister said that the new Labor-Greens-Independent government was not legitimate and that the idea of all parties getting together to smoke a peace pipe and sing 'Kum Ba Yah' would be treated with the contempt it deserved. The Liberal-Nationals were determined to be a 'ferocious opposition', their leader Tony Abbott said.

Despite two weeks of straight talking by the independents, it seemed that it was business as usual for some in the major parties. 'Kinder and gentler' had not even lasted a day and whether we Australians would engage more co-operatively in the debate on our future was an open question.

## Julia Gillard

Julia Gillard was born in Wales in 1961. Her family moved to Adelaide, South Australia, when she was five. After graduating from the University of Melbourne in 1986, she went to work for the law firm, Slater and Gordon, becoming a partner in 1990 at the age of 29. Entering parliament in 1998, she was sworn in as deputy Labor leader under prime minister Kevin Rudd in December 2007, the first woman to hold that position.

Rudd's declining public popularity and internal party bickering led Gillard to declare that 'a good government has lost its way' when, after many assertions that she would not contest the leadership, she suddenly did – and won.

She had been deeply popular as deputy prime minister, but Australia was less comfortable with their first female prime minister and with how she had got there. Gillard faced deeply entrenched sexism, culminating in a speech to parliament rallying against misogyny, prompted by Tony Abbott's statements and personal attacks on her.

Most ex-PMs fade away but after losing the 2013 election, Julia Gillard has become a strong advocate against misogyny, holding several prestigious international positions where she advocates for women, health and education. It seems likely that Gillard's contribution to continued social reform may have only just begun.

# THE INLAND TSUNAMI

2010 ended with a return to La Niña wet weather conditions. In November and December many areas saw up to six times their usual rainfall. On Christmas Day, 25 December 2010, tropical cyclone Tasha came inland south of Cairns bringing another 150–250 mm of rain to the east coast.

> **THE BOY HERO**
> **Thirteen-year old Jordan Rice told rescuers to save his younger brother first when their car was swept into flood-waters. Jordan's brother was rescued, but Jordan and his mother died before they could be reached.**

On 10 January 2011, a sudden thunderstorm caused a flash flood that inundated Toowoomba and a wall of water raced down the Lockyer Valley in an 'inland tsunami'. By 13 January more than 20,000 homes in Brisbane, Ipswich and southern Queensland were flooded.

More than 35 people were killed by floods that summer.

Brisbane had flooded many times before, and the 1974 flood had actually risen higher. But this flood harder, faster and more dangerous: since 1974 homes had been built in areas known to flood and all the roads, houses, car parks and other structures built since 1974 meant that the water couldn't soak down into the water table. Instead it rushed downhill becoming faster and deadly.

In Brisbane, a café, with its tables still set, floated down the river. So did a giant boardwalk, a vast length of wood and steel, threatening everything in its path, including homes along the riverbanks and the major bridge that connected north and south Brisbane. Only the valiant efforts of two tug-boat drivers managed to slowly nudge the vast structure into the middle of the river, saving lives and much of the city's economy.

But the floods also displayed the nation at its triumphant best too. As the water receded, my brother and nephew joined thousands of others with mops, spades and hoses. My nieces kept cooking during the clean up to keep volunteers fed and happy, linking via the internet with others to keep all the volunteers fed.

More than 60,000 volunteers registered that first day. Probably double that number turned up. But the most extraordinary thing was that none thought of themselves as heroes. They just did what was needed—and did it with jokes and laughter too. It was so very, very Australian. After Hurricane Katrina hit New Orleans in 2005, survivors were locked in football stadiums. But Australians held barbecues, cooked chocolate chip biscuits and then got out the mops and shovels.

I was proud to be part of my family in those weeks. I felt proud to be Australian, too.

## More Floods and Fire

On 2 February 2011 'Yasi', a Category 5 cyclone, crossed the far north Queensland coast near Mission Beach, between Cairns and Townsville, with wind gusts of 285 kilometres per hour. It shredded crops, smashed homes and marinas and tourist resorts.

In the south the south-eastern suburbs of Melbourne flooded and the town of Koo Wee Rup, 60 kilometres south-east of Melbourne, was evacuated.

All summer, parts of Queensland and northern New South Wales and Western Australia were flooded in turn. Farming and mining were badly hit; in many areas people lost their jobs or even worked for free till the damage could be repaired.

But parts of Australia still remained dry—and very hot.

Also in February, 50 houses were destroyed in bushfires in and around Perth. Australia had always been a land of extremes. But the extremes were becoming … extreme.

### The Deadly Ash from Far Away

**In June 2011, thousands of airline passengers across Australia were left stranded as flights had to be canceled as the ash cloud full of harsh and abrasive particles from Chile's Puyehue volcano would otherwise be sucked into their engines destroying them. The volcanic debris passed Australia once, and then again a week later stopping flights a second time before it dispersed.**

**It was yet another warning to Australia that we are part of a single small blue planet. All of us connected.**

## Polluters Will Pay!

In November 2011, the federal government passed legislation for a 'carbon tax' that would make polluting industries pay $23 per tonne of carbon emissions, with households compensated for any extra costs with tax cuts. Prime minister Julia Gillard said her Clean Energy Bills were a 'win for Australia's children', and reducing emissions would help slow down global warming.

In December, during UN Climate Change talks in Durban, South Africa, Australia and 189 other countries also agreed to a law that would slowly make the world's polluters slow the pace of climate change by 2020.

> **Australians still fought the Taliban in Afghanistan. In October 2011, three Australian soldiers were shot dead by a rogue soldier from the Afghan National Army. Another seven Australian soldiers were wounded and an Afghan interpreter also died. Eight other Australians were killed in Afghanistan that year.**

But before any polluters paid—or cut their emissions—the carbon tax was repealed by the next government under Tony Abbott. Despite growing global warming and damage from pollution, short-term jobs and profit—or even fewer jobs but larger company profits—was seen as more important than the long-term care for the world that young people would inherit.

## The Prime Minister Roundabout: Part 1

Australia once had a reputation for stability—prime ministers would stay in office till their party was voted out at the next election or until they died or retired.

'Who will challenge the PM?' had now become a game a bit like the fashionable reality shows on TV. Every week the media would come up with a new 'possible challenger'—and potential challengers and their supporters encouraged them.

In February 2012, foreign minister Kevin Rudd

resigned in order to mount a challenge to prime minister Gillard's leadership. He failed, but Australia—and the government—waited for the next challenge.

## The Boats Keep Coming

Australia had been a place of asylum for over 60,000 refugees. The refugees kept coming now, too, often in small decrepit boats in desperate danger of sinking, run by organised gangs of 'people smugglers' who were paid the full sum when the asylum seeker reached Australia.

In September 2012, after an independent panel recommended setting up holding centres in Nauru and Papua New Guinea, the government arranged to send the first group for processing in Nauru. Australia signed an agreement with Papua New Guinea to conduct offshore processing on Manus Island, part of Papua New Guinea's territory.

This arrangement would increasingly divide Australia—with those saying that all who wished to come should be allowed to, others fearing strangers from other cultures, while still more accepted the need for overseas centres where asylum seekers could be assessed to see if they were genuine refugees.

Still others, including the mayors of several country towns, argued that those seeking asylum should be placed in the community in regional areas where jobs could not be filled and schools needed more families with children to remain open. The asylum seekers could stay there until their cases could be judged, receiving good medical care and education, and given the chance to show they could be members of the community.

But the 'offshore solution' would remain.

**In August 2012, five more Australian soldiers were killed in Afghanistan in Australia's deadliest day in combat since the Vietnam War.**

# I Will Not Be Lectured By This Man

Julia Gillard and her government were becoming increasing unpopular with Australian voters. But in October 2012, Julia Gillard's speech denouncing opposition leader Tony Abbott as a misogynist went viral across the world, with newspapers and blogs applauding her condemnation of sexism: 'I will not be lectured about sexism and misogyny by this man, I will not.'

Overnight, 'Gillard' was one of the world's top trending words on social media.

The fight for equal rights for Australia women had seemed to have been won, with the right to vote, equal educational opportunities and anti-discrimination legislation enshrined in law. Women's sport was even shown on TV now! But women remained vulnerable to bullying, discrimination, lower pay for similar jobs—and violence.

In 2015, Rosie Battie was made Australian of the Year for her work defending women in situations of domestic violence. Rosie Battie's violent and mentally ill ex-partner had been legally forbidden from contacting her or their son, but twelve-year old Luke was killed in public at cricket practice by his father, despite all the legal protections that were supposed to exist. Too many abused women had nowhere to go now that so many women's refuges had closed due to funding cuts, nor were restraining orders policed despite the laws, nor did police resources meet the need to enforce court orders.

As the decade progressed the growing #MeToo movement condemned men in the entertainment industry who abused women—and got away with it because they were famous and powerful. In 2017, women in Australia and across the world began talking about the threats and intimidation they had suffered and been too scared to admit in case it cost them their jobs, future career opportunities or safety. More women came forward to speak about inequality in wages where women in the same jobs as men still received far less money.

## The Prime Minister Roundabout: Part 2

In June 2013, after months—or years—of accusations, undermining and speculation, Kevin Rudd challenged Julia Gillard as Labor leader and prime minister, as Labor ministers hoped that a new leader would increase the government's popularity. This time he won a parliamentary party vote—but lost the next federal election.

In September 2013, the Liberal-National Party Coalition, led by Tony Abbott, had a landslide victory.

## We Will Stop The Boats

The new government policies included instructing Australian naval vessels to intercept boats of migrants and asylum seekers and turning them back to Indonesia. The government stated that the numbers of boats attempting the crossing were greatly reduced, but at the same time they stopped making public the information about the numbers of boats that set out, were intercepted before they entered Australian waters or whether any boats arrived on Australian soil.

## TONY ABBOTT

Tony Abbott was born in 1957 in London and emigrated to Sydney, with his parents in 1960, where he attended Jesuit schools before enrolling at Sydney University. He graduated in economics and law, then attended Oxford as a Rhodes Scholar, studying politics and philosophy and gaining two 'Blues' for boxing.

A journalist, boxer, surf life saver, volunteer bush fire fighter and keen cyclist, the athletic Abbott also trained to be a Catholic priest. This would later lead to his political nickname 'The Mad Monk'. His strong religious views informed his policy decisions, issues including abortion, same-sex marriages and stem cell research. He also argued for tougher border controls, setting up a military-led border patrol called 'Operation Sovereign Borders'. A monarchist, he opposed any move for Australia to become a republic, instead reinstating the positions of knights and dames in the Order of Australia. He also dismissed scientific opinion on climate change as 'faddish', culminating in dismantling the Labor Party's attempt to address carbon emissions through an emissions trading scheme (the Carbon Tax).

## Terrorism In Australia

In the 1950s, Australia had been scared of Communism—the 'Reds Under the Beds'. Some of this fear was warranted. Much was not.

Now the great fear was terrorism, especially Islamic terrorism. In September 2014, Australia sent 600 military advisors to Iraq the help combat the Islamic State group. Back home police carried out the biggest ever series of anti-terrorism raids with reports that Islamic extremists were planning random killings. Fifteen people were arrested in raids in Sydney and Brisbane.

But these raids didn't stop the Lindt Café siege in December 2014, when Islamist Man Haron Monis took 18 people hostage in a Sydney CBD café. Two hostages and Man Haron Monis died when police stormed the café late that night, with much criticism levelled at the authorities over the ability of the police to handle hostage cases.

**In March 2014, Australia led the search for missing Malaysian Airlines plane MH370, thought to have been lost in the southern Indian Ocean. The mystery of what happened to the plane, which lost all contact soon after it took off, has still not been solved by 2018.**

Man Haron Monis was not a classic terrorist but a repeated abuser of women whose history of threats and actual violence was already known to police. Was this truly terrorism or another case of a mentally ill man causing yet more suffering and grief after police and the law had failed to carry out their legal obligations?

## The Prime Minister Roundabout: Part 2

Tony Abbott was losing popularity—and so was his government—especially when Mr Abbott tried to give Prince Phillip, the husband of Queen Elizabeth II, a newly reinstated Australian knighthood. In September 2015, communications minister Malcolm Turnbull replaced Mr Abbott as prime minister after a successful Liberal Party leadership challenge and announced a plan to hold an early a double dissolution election in June where elections would be held for the lower house and the whole Senate (rather than the more usual half Senate election). Mr Turnbull hoped that the swing towards

### Can You Read This?

**Australia had prided itself on being one of the best read and educated countries in the world. But by 2015 our position on world comparison charts was slipping badly, with one in five young people unable to read to the required internationally-agreed levels. Was the way reading was being taught the problem?**

**Even 20 years earlier, there had been many jobs for people who couldn't read. But now even people's friendships were conducted by text, email or social media. You now need to complete a safety check even to stack shelves in a supermarket; the person with a stop-go sign on the highway required a certificate to be accepted for the position. As machines, often remotely controlled, did more jobs the days of unskilled workers were vanishing. Education minister Simon Birmingham had a deep belief in the rights of all kids to learn to read. He wanted a five-minute informal test for all kids at the end of the first year at school to check that they were**

**learning what sounds matched the written word, but his proposal met with major opposition.**

**South Australia conducted a trial to see if using direct phonics instruction would help. By early 2018 it had not just dramatically helped kids learn to read, but had been enthusiastically endorsed by teachers. But would other states follow South Australia's lead?**

him in the polls would mean his government would win power in both houses.

They didn't. The early election in July 2016 saw the Liberal-National Party Coalition secure the narrowest possible majority in the House of Representatives—a majority of one seat. They could only pass legislation in the Senate with the help of of nine of the twenty 'cross benchers' now in the upper house. (The cross benchers sit at right angles to the government and opposition members and are either independents or representatives of minor parties.)

## Uluru statement

In May 2017 over 250 Aboriginal and Torres Strait Islander leaders met at the foot of Uluru in Central Australia on the lands of the Anangu people.

In the 'Uluru Statement from the Heart', the majority resolved to call for the establishment of a 'First Nations Voice' in the Australian Constitution and a Makarrata Commission to supervise a process of 'agreement-making' and 'truth-telling' between governments and Aboriginal and Torres Strait Islander peoples. Makarrata is a word in the language of the Yolngu people in Arnhem Land and it is more about acknowledging and healing than creating a formal treaty with Indigenous Australians.

The statement was criticised for the lack of representation

## MALCOLM TURNBULL

Turnbull was born in Sydney in 1954. Raised by his single father, he graduated in Arts and Laws from the University of Sydney where he was also involved in student politics and worked part-time as a journalist covering state politics. He then studied at Oxford as a Rhodes Scholar earning a Bachelor of Civil Law.

Turnbull became a highly successful and prominent barrister, then a merchant banker, investing in the IT company Ozemail at the beginning of the internet revolution. An avowed republican, he was chair of the Australian Republican Movement from 1994 to 2000.

Malcolm Turnbull was elected to the House of Representatives as the Liberal member for Wentworth at the federal election in 2004. He became the leader of opposition in 2008. He lost that post to Tony Abbott in 2009 by one vote over his support for the Labor government's carbon pollution reduction scheme that was designed to combat climate change. In September 2015, Turnbull again ran for leadership of the parliamentary Liberal Party and defeated Abbott by ten votes, this time becoming the prime minister.

of some Indigenous groups and for a lack of fine detail; other members of the Convention walked out in opposition to the statement, but across Australia there was also widespread support for a form of legal recognition. Prime minister Turnbull reacted by saying that the Constitution could only be changed by a referendum and he was not confident that it would receive a sufficient measure of support. At the time of writing, no such referendum has been suggested or supported by the government.

## Who Can We Marry?

In an historical postal survey in December 2017, 61.6 per cent of Australians who voted in a non-compulsory, non-binding postal survey wanted equality for same sex marriages. The debate was anguish for many, with vitriol expressed on both sides of the campaign, but afterwards the feeling was one of triumph not just for the results, but because for the first time the Australian people had cast postal votes on a single issue about which they cared—and their wishes had been made law.

## How Do You Know That?

It was a campaign that was fought increasingly on social media. Only a decade earlier political campaigns were carried out with TV, radio and newspaper ads and debates. Before that candidates and their supporters relied on knocking on

**In August 2016 Human Rights Watch and Amnesty International accused the Australian government of abusing refugees and asylum seekers at its camp on Nauru. Prime minister Malcolm Turnbull stated that the claims would be investigated. Regularly, however, there continued to be stories of suicides, cruelty, assault, injustice and tragedy at both Manus and Naura.**

**Australia finally closed the controversial asylum seeker detention centre on Papua New Guinea's Manus Island, but said none of the 850 people would be resettled in Australia. Many were sent to Nauru. At the time of writing, others still waited in desperate conditions in Papua New Guinea, classified as refugees but with nowhere to go, even though New Zealand had offered to resettle 150 of the refugees, but prime minister Turnbull refused the offer. As I write this, 1,250 refugees are supposed to be resettled in the US but so far only 50 have actually been assessed and accepted.**

doors or speaking to crowds from the back of trucks.

But increasingly newspapers were losing readers to online sites where people could browse news from all over the world on free sites or ones with a small annual fee. TV viewing was down too, as viewers switched to streaming services where they could watch all of a show's episodes in one binge instead of waiting for weekly episodes—and having them interrupted by TV ads and scheduling.

But advertising had subsidised news reports and online advertising wasn't paying enough to do the same kind of in-depth investigation. Between 2014 and 2018 even the publically-funded network the Australian Broadcasting Corporation (ABC) decreased its news and factual investigation coverage by 60 per cent. Slowly journalists and investigators used 'crowd funding' to pay them to investigate major new stories. Charities, too, found funds using social media.

The way Australians linked together—and our relations with like-minded people across the world—was changing fast.

## Would You Like A Drone With That?

Unskilled jobs were vanishing but new technology was exciting. By 2018 prototypes of driverless cars had been tested and semi-driverless cars—ones where computers assisted the driver to turn corners efficiently or steer in hard conditions—were available, though only in more expensive cars.

Paper maps were vanishing too. Nearly all cars now used satellite navigation (sat navs) where a computer voice gave directions. Those who didn't have one installed in their car could use the sat nav on their mobile phone—and take a selfie when they got there.

Fifty years earlier a photograph was only taken to record important events like birthdays or family reunions or once-a-year school photos. Now bloggers and Instagrammers took photos of their meals, their clothes, or their make-up daily or even more often for their followers (highly successful bloggers could have many thousands followers)—and many of those received money from advertisers on their sites.

Eating out was suddenly becoming 'eating in'. Uber and similar companies were challenging taxis and buses with part-time drivers using their own cars and a mobile phone app to connect with passengers. Now, with Uber Eats you could choose from a restaurant's online menu and for a few dollars have it delivered to you.

Restaurants began to cut down the number of tables in their actual establishments and increase their staff for preparing delivered meals. Other businesses sprang up with no seating, preparing meals for customers they would never see.

To begin with, part-time drivers delivered these in their own cars. But by 2018 businesses overseas, and even in Australia, were beginning to use drones to fly meals to their customers by-passing traffic. Drones were increasingly used to photograph news events, weddings, real estate or just for fun as well as for scientific surveys.

Was the day coming soon when instead of a driverless car, people might travel in a driverless, remotely-controlled drone?

## Goodbye Malls?

The age of online shopping had begun. Malls were closing all across the US, and shops were closing in Australian malls and shopping centres too. Why battle traffic when you could shop online at home, at work or even on public transport? In the major cities and many regional centres even supermarket shopping could be done online.

Instead the shopping experience was changing. Artisanal foods or clothes shops were opening that offered a different retail experience offering fun as well as product. Shopping became a hobby for many, so much so that for the first time charities were turning away previously worn clothes and other goods donated to them. A fashion blogger—or someone who followed them—might wear an outfit once or three times, then give (or throw) it away. Op-shoppers could buy a $1,000 outfit for $10 if they looked hard enough.

In the 1920s, the new 'conveniences' like irons and fridges and vacuum cleaners were meant to last a lifetime—or even two. Now a three-to-six-year life was considered reasonable. Even those who didn't like to shop had to shop, as what they bought was so badly made, often with planned obsolescence built into the design where even a computer that still worked had to be replaced because it could no longer run the most recent software.

Most people even booked holidays online, instead of physically going to a travel agent. Online sites offered rooms in people homes to stay in, instead of hotel rooms, or even whole houses or apartments could be rented. This brought income for people who would otherwise find it hard to afford to pay a mortgage, but also brought problems as tourists—or tourist parties—moved into residential areas.

## Life Is Good

By 2018 life was good for most Australians—after all, Melbourne had just been nominated as the world's most livable city—except for the facts that:

- 42,000 homeless people had no bed to sleep in at night, more than twice the number there had been in 2014;
- many Indigenous communities were still battling problems of few or no services that people in cities and most country towns took for granted, as well

as deep casual racial prejudice;

- the number of drug addicts was increasing as new 'designer' drugs appeared on the streets; and
- a growing number of mentally ill people were struggling with less and less funding for hospital beds, supported accommodation or treatment.

There was a growing number of elderly people too. The 'boomer' generation born after World War II were now becoming old, too. Despite nursing homes and retirement villages charging more per day than many five-star hotels, the average money spent on all the meals per day in 2018 was just over $6, less than half of what it had been two years before and not much more than the regular $4.50 price of a take-away coffee. Residents starved or grew malnourished on slop and fish fingers. Qualified staff were fired and replaced with poorly paid, minimally-trained staff. Each week the media carried yet another horror story of elderly people with bed sores, undiagnosed and untreated illnesses and general neglect.

Public surgery lists averaged a three-year wait, which would have been longer if others on the list didn't die before they could be given the medical treatment they needed.

Australia had prided itself on being a land of mateship and giving people a fair go. Sometimes it even had been.

That had changed.

## New Power!

Throughout 2016 South Australia was hit by a series of major power blackouts—their power grid couldn't cope with people's increased needs for air-conditioning, as well as the demands made by new industries. In September, violent storms brought high winds, several small tornadoes and over 80,000 lightning strikes bringing the state-wide system to a standstill as major transmission lines were also brought down and the interconnector from Victoria was tripped.

American alternative power innovator, billionaire Elon Musk, bet $50 million that he could install a battery farm to solve the problems within 100 days. In fact he did it in 63 days. The Tesla system at Hornsdale was designed to allow wind energy to be delivered to the grid at any time, whether the wind was blowing or not.

Within a few days the system was tested and was an overwhelming success and it enabled South Australia to augment Victoria's power supply in the first week of December when a heat wave meant the Victorian grid couldn't cope.

Scientifically and technically, the country's energy problems could be solved. But would industry—and politicians who wanted industry support—accept that the world had changed?

In February 2018, it was announced that the coal-fired Liddell Power Station in New South Wales would be closed in 2020; it was old and its owner had decided to move to more reliable, less polluting, renewable power systems like

## Mad Times For Millennials

**'Millennials' was the name given to people who became adults after the year 2000. Millennials were more likely than others in the work populations to have only part time jobs, or a casual job. Rising house prices and rising rents meant they were less likely to ever be able to buy a home. Millennials also had to pay more for education than any generation since 1973.**

**But millennials also had chances in new industries and technologies than no generation ever had before.**

solar and wind. Prime minster Turnbull threatened legal action to stop the plant from closing even though it would by then be past its safe and efficient operating life. Why? Was it a longing for 'the ways things used to be' now that change was happening so quickly? Or a wish to please coal mining companies? Or a bit of both?

In February 2018, the SA government planned to install solar panels with battery storage in 50,000 low-income households, lowering power bills for those households by up to a third and making system-wide power blackouts even less likely. But in March 2018, the new SA Liberal Party government said it was not bound to the plan.

The world was changing—fast. Could we change fast enough to adapt to the changes?

## Our Planet Warms–<br>We Do Not Stand Alone

For over 60,000 years Indigenous, and then early colonial Australia, was 'the land at the end of the world'. Our distance kept us relatively safe from plagues and even the worst effects of wars.

But by 2018, Australia had become linked by social media, allowing ordinary Australians to chat, exchange news and research instantaneously with all those across our planet.

But as the planet warmed, ocean levels rose and weather

became more extreme due to humans warming the planet with coal-fire-powered electricity stations, buildings that required year-round heating and cooling, car vehicle exhausts and much more. Australia no longer had distance to protect it from the consequences of these choices and actions.

As the world's jet stream slowed, cold or warm air lingered longer. Rain, heat, or snow lingered longer. A rainstorm was more likely to be a flood; a heat wave lasted for weeks instead of days, bringing the threat of bushfire. Rainfall events often saw large amounts of rain fall in a short period of time followed by hot, dry periods.

The warm Atlantic current linked to severe and abrupt changes in the climate was at its weakest in at least 1,600 years, which was as long as it could be measured. If—or when—it failed, North America and parts of Europe would face catastrophic cold. And the rest of the world?

The polar icecaps were melting far faster than predicted only ten years before. The scientific consensus that 'the world is warming due to human industry' was now warning that 'things are changing faster but we don't know how fast or how, or when'. The changes were coming too fast, with too little money for research to know the details. The Australian government seemed determined to ignore the reports of its climate scientists and meteorologists.

April 2018 was the warmest on record in Australia.

Bushfires were no longer a rare tragedy—on 18 March 2018 70 homes were burnt with almost no warning on an unseasonably hot, dry, windy day at Tathra on the NSW south coast, while on the same day another 18 houses and many more outbuildings were lost in south-western Victoria. In April another massive bushfire threatened southern Sydney suburbs. In this new world of climate change, bushfires, cyclones, tornadoes and violent storm surges might come at any time.

Some very expensive real estate along the east coast had rapidly lost value over the past decade as the beaches eroded. Homes were now perched above gaping holes with water washing below, as seawalls crumbled into the sea during storms and high tides. Much of the millionaire real estate in New South Wales and Queensland consisted of canal developments only 60 centimetres or so above sea level. While seas were still only rising at about 3 millimetres per year, storm surges were becoming greater, sweeping away coastal land and homes.

## Advance Adani?

All through 2017 and 2018, debate raged about a proposed coal mine in the north of the Galilee Basin of Central Queensland, which would utilise both open-cut and underground methods. The proposal came from Adani Mining, a part of India's Adani Group. The federal and state governments had promised over $1 billion to help the Adani Group to create jobs in the economically depressed Townsville area.

But could more jobs be created with a billion dollars invested in something less polluting? Was the mine even commercially viable if it needed so much money from the Australian people/taxpayers to build it? What about pollution on the Great Barrier Reef, one of Australia's greatest tourist destinations and on the World Heritage register? Pollution from ports, farming and leaks from ships as well as the effects of global warming, were already killing the coral, 'bleaching' it so that 30-40 per cent of the reef was no longer the wonderland of colours and fish that tourists had flown across the world to see.

Promises were made and withdrawn—and so were proposals for the Adani project. Public opinion was strongly against any taxpayer money going to help the company. A smaller majority were against the coal mine no matter how it was funded, as it would add to the world's carbon pollution as it was burnt to provide electricity and subsequent global warming. Stop Adani protests were held across the country. By mid-2018 it was hard to say what would happen to the project.

## What Now?

The world was in trouble. In April 2018, a major UN-backed biodiversity study revealed that unsustainable exploitation of the natural world threatened the food and water security of billions of people. Too many people living in the First World were consuming too much of the world's finite resources and most of the developing world wanted to consume even more.

Fisheries in the Asia-Pacific were predicted to decline to zero by 2048; fresh, unpolluted water in the Americas was less than half what there had been in the 1950s; and 42 per cent of land species in Europe had declined in the past decade.

Most Australians were comfortably well off and probably among the safest in the world. Billionaires bought land in Australia, especially in Tasmania, as well as New Zealand, in case a nuclear war broke out between the US and China or North Korea or over the Middle East; or in case a new pandemic swept the world or a solar flare took out the world's satellite communications systems (that banking and power systems all depended on) and as the fresh water supplies dried up in South Africa, parts of the US, India and the Middle East. Some simply wanted clean, non-polluted air and fresh food.

## What Comes Next?

In the past 50 years, the world changed from steam trains to space stations, from letters to mobile phones. Every decade brought brilliant inventions that made our lives better—but also many that hurt our planet, as more people consumed more, and polluted more. Science and technology had also become far in advance of most governments' ability to control or to adapt to them.

But people could also learn about their world, its problems and solutions, more easily than ever before. They could campaign for the things they think are right more easily too.

The 'Millennials'—those who became adult or were born in the 'new' millennium—faced the challenges of casual instead of permanent jobs and house prices too high for many to buy or even rent. But they were also the most educated generation in human history, the best connected by computers and mobile phones, a generation who could call up all the information on a subject in ten minutes instead of the years or decades it might have taken their ancestors.

And this generation were showing they were prepared to find new and visionary solutions to the world's problems, too, from saving endangered species to extending human life, caring for our planet, or reaching the stars. The future might not be easy, but those who accept the challenges of the future will not be bored.

The next chapters of our history were going to be the most exciting yet—and they are up to you.

# Bibliography

Brett, J (ed)1997, *Political Lives*, Sydney, Allen & Unwin.

Brett, J 2005, Relaxed and Comfortable: the Liberal Party's Australia, *Quarterly Essay* no.19, Melbourne, Black Inc.

Brett, J 2007, Exit Right—the Unravelling of John Howard, *Quarterly Essay* no.28, Melbourne, Black Inc

Dodson, M 2010, Australian of the Year: Speech to the National Press Club http://www.australianoftheyear.org.au/pages/page525.asp

Flannery, T 2008, Now or Never—a Sustainable Future for Australia? *Quarterly Essay* no.31, Melbourne, Black Inc.

Grattan, M (ed) 2000, *Australian Prime Ministers*, Sydney, New Holland.

Hanson, P 1996 Maiden Speech in the House of Representatives http://australianpolitics.com/parties/onenation/96-09-10hanson-first-speech.shtml

Hawke RJL The Bob Hawke Prime Ministerial Library http://www.unisa.edu.au/hawkecentre/library/new.asp

Keating, P The Hon Paul Keating Official Website http://www.keating.org.au/main.cfm

Marr, D 2010, Power Trip: The Political Journey of Kevin Rudd, *Quarterly Essay no.38*, Melbourne, Black Inc.

Marr, D & M Wilkinson 2003, *Dark Victory*, Sydney, Allen & Unwin.

Oakes, L & D Solomon 1973, *The Making of an Australian Prime Minister*, Melbourne, Cheshire.

Randall, B 2003, *Songman: the Story of an Aboriginal Elder of Uluru*, Sydney, ABC Books

Randall, B & M Hogan 2006, *Kanyini* (film).

Rudd K 2008, Apology 13 February http://www.smh.com.au/articles/2008/02/13/1202760379056.html

Watson, D 2002, *Recollections of a Bleeding Heart: A Portrait of Paul Keating PM*, Sydney, Knopf.

Wesley, M 2007, *The Howard Paradox: Australian Diplomacy in Asia 1996-2006*, Sydney, ABC Books.

Whitlam, EG 1979, *The Truth of the Matter*, Melbourne, Penguin.

# INDEX

*The Indigenous people of Australia have lived here for tens of thousands of years. They survived the ice age and ancient global warming. They saw oceans sink and oceans rise. They watched the mega-beasts disappear and dingoes arrive. Theirs is the oldest civilisation in the world.*

*Then along came the Dutch. And the Portuguese. And the British. Things would never be the same again.*

*It was the craziest, wildest and most daring expedition the world had seen.*

*Eleven ships with nearly 1500 people travelled 25 000 kilometres to the other side of the world. But what did they find when they arrived?*

*Cannibal convicts, murdering squatters, sea captains who kidnapped their crew, poor farmers forced off their land—they had all come to the colonies of New South Wales and Van Diemen's Land to make better lives for themselves. And now there were new colonies and farms spreading around Australia.*

*For 60,000 years the rest of the world had pretty much left Australia and its Aboriginal nations alone.*
*Then it became a home for Britain's criminals and poor.*
*Now a con man had found gold and suddenly everyone was heading to Australia: adventurers, revolutionaries, camels . . .*
*Australia would never be the same.*

*The Australian colonies had come a long way since they were a dump for grim crims and convicts. Life was comfortable—at least for some. But soon drought would send swaggies waltzing their matildas along the roads, and bad times would make politicians dream of uniting the country into one nation.*

*And then a far-off war would create a different kind of digger. What they brought back home would make greater changes to Australia than gold ever did.*

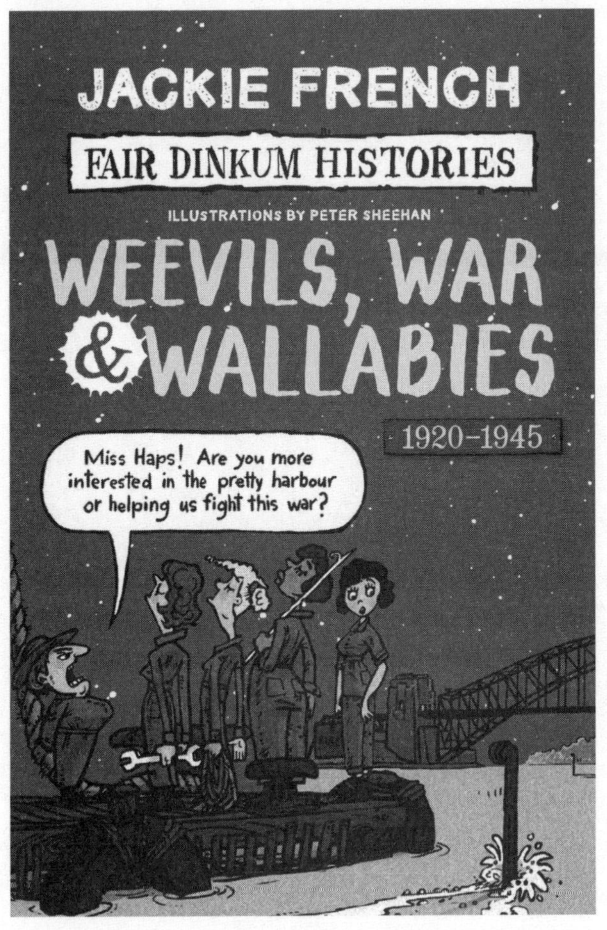


*The diggers of World War I came back to an Australia still divided by class, gender and race. At least the country could celebrate for a time during the 'roaring twenties'. But then the stock market crashed and we were plunged into the Great Depression. Unemployment and evictions sent men out 'on the wallaby'. Times were tough, and they'd only get tougher with the start of another world war, this time much closer to home . . .*

*World War II was over, and it was a good time to be Australian. Rock 'n' roll, TV and the Olympics had come down under. But underneath it all was the menace of the Cold War, and then came the horrors of Korea and Vietnam. Why couldn't we all just get along?*